SMALL *Oxford* BOOKS

FOX-HUNTING

SMALL *Oxford* BOOKS

━━━━━━━━━━ ❧❧❧ ━━━━━━━━━━

FOX-HUNTING

━━━━━━━━━━ ❧❧❧ ━━━━━━━━━━

Compiled by
SARA AND RAYMOND CARR

Oxford New York
OXFORD UNIVERSITY PRESS
1982

Oxford University Press, Walton Street, Oxford OX2 6DP

London Glasgow New York Toronto
Delhi Bombay Calcutta Madras Karachi
Kuala Lumpur Singapore Hong Kong Tokyo
Nairobi Dar es Salaam Cape Town
Melbourne Auckland

and associates in
Beirut Berlin Ibadan Mexico City Nicosia

British Library Cataloguing in Publication Data

Fox-hunting.—(Small Oxford books)
1. Fox-hunting
I. Carr, Sara II. Carr, Raymond
799.2'5974442   SK285
ISBN 0-19-214140-6

Set by Western Printing Services Ltd.
Printed in Great Britain by
Hazell Watson & Viney Limited
Aylesbury, Bucks

Introduction

By the mid-eighteenth century the fox had replaced the deer and the hare as the chief 'beast of venery' in England. By 1800, what had been the affair of a few aristocrats or the squire and his friends had become, in the grass countries of the Midlands, a sport capable of attracting hundreds of followers. Most visitors to Leicestershire came for the excitements of the fast runs made possible by the technical innovations associated with Hugo Meynell, Master of the Quorn 1753–1800. By the 1860s Anthony Trollope could refer to fox-hunting as 'the national sport'. The attractions of Melton Mowbray never weakened the vitality of fox-hunting in 'the provinces' – rural England as a whole.

Railways cut up hunting countries into 'a vast grid-iron', a process to be completed by the motorway, but improved transport allowed enthusiasts to hunt in Leicestershire in the morning and get back for dinner in London; it expanded geographically a pastime that had already expanded socially beyond the rural establishment and the local farmers on whose tolerance of hunters crashing over their land the whole sport depended and still depends. This twin expansion – social and geographical – is revealed by the fact that both Lord Althorp, a great aristocrat and a leader of the Whig party in the 1830s and Mr Enoch Powell, who was once a University Professor, hunted in Leicestershire by train from London. The successor to the Regency Bucks who gambled at the 'Club' in Melton Mowbray is Victor Lowndes, former Director of the Playboy Club, who goes out with his local pack.

We have tried to illustrate the changing composition of the hunting field and the excitements which can attract to a sport, under fire politically by the left, an estimated 50,000 subscribers and a million foot and car followers.

Already by the 1830s fox-hunting had seen the rise of sporting journalists like the great snob 'Nimrod' (C. J. Apperley) and produced in Robert Smith Surtees a novelist whose characters – John Jorrocks, Mr Sponge and Facey Romford – can rival those of the urban Dickens. Anthony Trollope, himself a passionate fox-hunter, introduced hunting scenes into nearly all his novels; in Siegfried Sassoon's *Memoirs of a Fox-Hunting Man* the sport inspired a work of genius, perhaps the only book that can hope to explain the attractions (and limitations) of fox-hunting to the indifferent.

No book can hope to convert the 'antis'. There are the humanitarians who have always attacked fox-hunting because it is cruel. There are the radicals enraged by what they consider, in the words of a President of the Junior Common Room of that great nursery of MFHs, Christ Church, Oxford, a 'bourgeois' sport. Fox-hunting has always been a controversial sport. We have presented both the attack – usually misconceived – and the defence – usually lame.

S. & R. C.

Fox-hunting, however lively and animating it may be in the field, is but a dull, dry subject to write upon.

Peter Beckford, *Thoughts upon Hunting*, 1781

The Fox

Thief o' the world.

R. S. Surtees

A shrewd and fell thief.

Reynart the Foxe, tr. by William Caxton, 14th century

Most cunning among all the beasts of the field is the Fox.

Appian, *Cynegetica*, 3rd century AD

If an artist was desired to paint the most perfect animal in the shape of a quadruped, it would be not *a* fox, but *the* fox; for they are all so nearly alike in point of symmetry; and, on examination, it will be found that no animal has so much muscle in proportion to its size, and the bone, like that of a thorough-bred horse, is like ivory: in point of strength of loins, nothing can exceed it.

Tom Smith, Master of the Craven 1829–33,
Extracts from the Diary of a Huntsman, 1833

An early and misleading description.

His nature in many respects is like that of a *Wolf*; for they bring as many Cubs at a Litter one as the other: but thus they differ; the *Fox* Litters deep under the ground, so doth not the *Wolf*.

A Bitch-*Fox* is hardly to be taken when she is bragged and with Cub; for then she will lie near her Burrow, into which she runs upon the hearing of the least noise: And indeed at any time it is somewhat difficult; for the *Fox* (and so the *Wolf*) is a very subtle crafty Creature.

Fox-Hunting is very pleasant; for by reason of his strong hot scent he maketh an excellent Cry: And as his scent is hottest at hand, so it dies soonest. Besides, he never flies far before the Hounds, trusting not on his Legs, Strength or Champion Ground, but strongest Coverts. When he can no longer stand up before the Hounds, he then taketh Earth, and then must he be digged out.

If Grey-hounds course him on a Plain, his last refuge is to piss on his Tail, and flap it in their faces as they come near him; sometimes squirting his thicker Excrement upon them, to make them give over the Course or Pursuit.

When a Bitch-*Fox* goes a clicketing and seeketh for a Dog, she crieth with a hollow Voice, not unlike the howling of a mad Dog; and in the same manner she cries when she misseth any of her Cubs: but never makes any cry at all when she is killing, but defends herself to the last gasp.

A *Fox* will prey upon any thing he can overcome, and feeds upon all sorts of Carrion; but their Dainties, and the Food which they most delight in, is Poultry. They are very destructive and injurious to *Coney*-Warrens, and will sometimes kill *Hares* by deceit and subtilty, and not by swift running.

The *Fox* is taken with Hounds, Grey-hounds, Terriers, Nets, and Gins.

Nicholas Cox, *The Gentleman's Recreation*, 1674

Then Dan Russél the fox stert up at once . . .
His colour was betwixt yelwe and red;
And tipped was his tail, and both his eres
With black, unlike the remenant of his heres.
His snout was smal, with glowing eyen twey . . .
A col fox, ful of sleigh iniquitee.

Chaucer, 'The Nun's Priest's Tale,'
The Canterbury Tales, c. 1387

. . . a magnificent fellow in a spotless suit of fur crossed
the ride before him at a quiet, stealing, listening sort of
pace, and gave a whisk of his well-tagged brush on
entering the copse-wood.

R. S. Surtees, *Handley Cross*, 1843

*In the seventeenth century foxes were hunted 'under-
ground'. Here is Nicholas Cox's account of training a
terrier put in with a badger or a fox:*

Cut away the nether jaw, but meddle not with the
other, leaving the upper to show the fury of the Beast,
although it can do no harm therewith . . . Here note
that, instead of cutting away the Jaw, it will be every
whit as well to break out all his Teeth, to prevent him
biting the terriers.

The Gentleman's Recreation, 1674

The fox, the great dark dog, lay dozing,
His gold eyes opening and closing;
He slept no longer as a log
But half awake, the great dark dog.
He lay restored, he lay well rested,
He lay, his dinner well digested,
He lay as fit as any fiddle.
Dry as a bannock on a griddle
He curled half napping and half sleeping,
And all his senses in his keeping.

Patrick Chalmers, *The Horn*, 1937

The death of a fox by any other means than hunting was unnatural to fox-hunters. Assheton Smith, one of the greatest nineteenth-century Masters, was observed to pale at the breakfast table :

The ladies present, supposing some great European calamity had occurred, hastily asked what was the matter, when he replied, looking over his spectacles: 'By Jove, a dog fox has been burnt to death in a barn'.

J. E. Eardley Wilmot, *Reminiscences of the late Thomas Assheton Smith*, 1862

Vulpicide, the deliberate killing of a fox, other than by hunting, was, to fox-hunters, an unspeakable outrage.

In a visit to a friend, at a great town in the North, I accompanied him to the public bowling-green, where I saw a very genteel looking man, who seemed to be shunned by every body. By accident, entering into conversation with him, I found him a very well-informed, polite, and agreeable gentleman. On my way home, I could not help taking notice of what I had observed; and enquired of my friend the cause of this gentleman being thus evidently disregarded. 'Cause enough,' answered he; 'that fellow is the greatest scoundrel upon earth.' – 'What has he done?' said I – 'Has he any unnatural vices? Has he debauched the wife or daughter of his friend? Or is he a bad husband or father?' – 'We don't trouble ourselves about his amours or connections,' peevishly answered my friend; 'but to do the fellow justice there is nothing of that – he is besides both a good husband and father.' 'What then, has he committed a murder, or been guilty oi treason?' 'No,' added my friend – 'besides, we have nothing to do with his quarrels, and don't trouble our heads with his party; we have nothing to say against him on those subjects.' 'What then, in the name oi Fortune, can it be! Is he a cheat, a black-legs, or an usurer?' 'No, no!' replied my friend, 'no such thing; but if you will have it, know then, that good-looking plausible villain, in his own farm-yard, shot a bitch-fox, big with young.' – Recollecting that my friend, and most of the gentlemen on the green, were staunch fox-hunters, my wonder ceased.

Francis Goose, *The Grumbler*, 1796

There is something doubtless absurd in the intensity of the worship paid to the fox by hunting communities. The animal becomes sacred, and his preservation is a religion. His irregular destruction is a profanity, and words spoken to his injury are blasphemous. Not long since a gentleman shot a fox running across a woodland ride in a hunting country. He had mistaken it for a hare, and had done the deed in the presence of keepers, owner, and friends. His feelings were so acute and his remorse so great that, in their pity, they had resolved to spare him; and then, on the spot, entered into a solemn compact that no one should be told. Encouraged by the forbearing tenderness, the unfortunate one ventured to return to the house of his friend, the owner of the wood, hoping that, in spite of the sacrilege committed, he might be able to face a world that would be ignorant of his crime. As the vulpicide, on the afternoon of the day of the deed, went along the corridor to his room, one maid-servant whispered to another, and the poor victim of an imperfect sight heard the words – 'That's he as shot the fox!' The gentleman did not appear at dinner, nor was he ever again seen in those parts.

Anthony Trollope, *Phineas Redux*, 1874

To the despair of Masters and Huntsmen some fox-hunters are overcome with a sudden sympathy with the hunted fox. In Siegfried Sassoon's autobiographical novel this spontaneous sympathy overcomes George Sherston.

Where we rode the winter sunshine was falling warmly into the wood, though the long grass in the shadows was still flaked with frost. A blackbird went scolding away among the undergrowth, and a jay was setting up a clatter in an ivied oak. Some distance off Jack Pitt was shouting 'Yoi-over' and tooting his horn in a leisurely sort of style. Then we turned a corner and came upon Denis. He had pulled his pony across the path, and his face wore a glum look which, as I afterwards learnt to know, merely signified that, for the moment, he had found nothing worth thinking about. The heavy look lifted as I approached him with a faltering smile, but he nodded at me with blunt solemnity, as if what thoughts he had were elsewhere.

'Morning. So you managed to get here.' That was all I got by way of greeting. Somewhat discouraged, I could think of no conversational continuance. But Dixon gave him the respectful touch of the hat due to a 'proper little sportsman' and, more enterprising than I, supplemented the salute with 'Bit slow in finding this morning, sir?'

'Won't be much smell to him when they do. Sun's too bright for that.' He had the voice of a boy, but his manner was severely grown up.

There was a brief silence, and then his whole body seemed to stiffen as he stared fixedly at the undergrowth. Something rustled the dead leaves; not more than ten yards from where we stood, a small russet animal stole out on to the path and stopped for a photographic instant to take a look at us. It was the first time I had ever seen a fox, though I have seen a great many since – both alive and dead. By the time he had slipped out of sight again I had just begun to realize what it was that had looked at me with such human alertness. Why I should have behaved as I did I will not attempt to explain, but when Denis stood up in his stirrups and emitted a shrill 'Huick-holler', I felt spontaneously alarmed for the future of the fox.

'Don't do that; they'll catch him!' I exclaimed.

The words were no sooner out of my mouth than I knew I had made another fool of myself. Denis gave me one blank look and galloped off to meet the huntsman, who could already be heard horn-blowing in our direction in a maximum outburst of energy.

Memoirs of a Fox-Hunting Man, 1928

Writing in the Nineteenth Century, *even so seasoned a fox-hunter as Sir William Bromley Davenport acknowledged this sympathy with the hunted animal:*

I confess, when I alone have come across the hiding place of a 'beaten' fox, and he has, so to speak, confided his secret to me with big upturned and indescribably appealing eye, it has been sacred to me; I have retired softly, and rejoiced with huge joy when the huntsman at last calls away his baffled pack.

Hounds

D'ye ken that bitch whose tongue was death?
D'ye ken her sons of peerless faith?
D'ye ken that a fox, with his last breath,
  Curs'd them all as he died in the morning?

Yes I ken John Peel and Ruby too,
Ranter and Royal and Bellman as true,
From the drag to the chase, from the chase to the view,
  From the view to the death in the morning.

From the 'definitive' version of the best
loved of hunting songs, by John Woodcock Graves, 1866

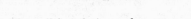

The breeding of hounds is at the very centre of fox-hunting.

Mind my successor never loses sight of Ranter or his blood.

Dying words of Will Smith, the Brockelsby
Huntsman, killed in the hunting field.

Both the beauty and adaptation of hounds to their function have, from Shakespeare to John Masefield, inspired poets.

HIPPOLYTA.   Never did I hear
  Such gallant chiding; for, besides the groves,
  The skies, the fountains, every region near
  Seem'd all one mutual cry: I never heard
  So musical a discord, such sweet thunder.
William Shakespeare, *A Midsummer Night's Dream*, 1600

Squire Somerville (1675–1742) was a Fellow of New College, Oxford. He describes the perfect hound.

See there, with countenance blythe,
And with a courtly grin, the fawning hound
Salutes them cow'ring; his wide op'ning nose
Upwards he curls, and his large sloe-black eyes
Melt in soft blandishments and humble joy:
His glossy skin, or yellow pied, or blue,
In lights or shades, by Nature's pencil drawn,
Reflects the various tints: his ears and legs
Fleckt here and there in gay enamel'd pride,
Rival the speckled pard; his rush-grown tail
O'er his broad back, bends in an ample arch,
On shoulders clean upright and firm he stands:
His round cat feet, straight hams, and widespread thighs
And his low drooping chest, confess his speed,
His strength, his wind, or on the steepy hill
Or far extended plain; on every part
So well proportioned, that the nicer skill
Of Phidias himself can't blame thy choice.
Of such compose thy pack.

And hounds working.

See! how they range
Dispers'd, how busily this way and that
They cross, examining with curious nose
Each likely haunt. Hark! on the drag I hear
Their doubtful notes, preluding to a cry
More nobly full, and swell'd with every mouth.

The Chace, 1735

An eighteenth-century description of a bad start :

The morning wakes, the huntsman sounds,
At once rush forth the joyful hounds;
They seek the wood with eager pace,
Through bush, through brier explore the chase;
Now scattered wide they try the plain,
And snuff the dewy turf in vain.

What care, what industry, what pains!
What universal silence reigns!

John Gay, 'The Hound and the Huntsman' from *Fables*, 1727

*The building of magnificent kennels to house expensive
hounds was attacked as an outrage to the squalidly housed
rural poor. Squire Somerville's counsels, characteristic of
eighteenth-century moderation, were forgotten in the
Victorian* blütezeit *of fox-hunting.*

Let no Corinthian Pillars prop the Dome,
A vain Expense, or charitable Deeds
Better dispos'd, to clothe the tatter'd Wretch
Who shrinks beneath the Blast, to feed the Poor
Pinch'd with afflictive Want: For Use, not State,
Gracefully plain, let each Apartment rise.
Bestrew the Pavement, and no half-pick'd Bones,
To kindle fierce Debate, or to disgust
That nicer Sense, on which the Sportsman's Hope
And all his future Triumphs must depend.
Soon as the growling Pack with eager Joy
Have lapp'd their smoking Viands, Morn or Eve,
From the full Cistern lead the ductile Streams,
To wash thy Court well-pav'd, nor spare thy Pains,
For much to Health will Cleanliness avail.
Seek'st thou for Hounds to climb the rocky Steep,
And brush th' entangled Covert, whose nice Scent
O'er greasy Fallows and frequented Roads
Can pick the dubious Way? Banish far off
Each noisome Stench, let no offensive Smell
Invade thy wide Inclosure, but admit
The nitrous Air and purifying Breeze.

William Somerville, *The Chace*, 1735

*Individual hounds became objects of near worship and
anthropomorphic fantasy. The introduction of smaller,*

white Welsh hounds revolutionized hound breeding in the twentieth century.

But there was Conqueror. After all, whatever happened, there was old Conqueror. He was Welsh, untarnished white, and shaggy as a Highland bull. He had a massive skull, and out of this tangled forehead his amber eyes, steady and penetrative, examined the world with the fierce austerity of a Mr Gladstone.

He had been as a puppy a source of intense pride in the primitive farmstead where he was walked. John, the old kennelman, had diagnosed him as 'one of the stand-offish sort,' and he was. Conqueror never asked for trouble, in kennel or out, but he also saw he never got it. For all his aloof and magnificent detachment he had an eye for the corner of the sleeping-bench. His only source of grievance was that, owing to a splendid appetite and digestion, he was invited in late to the trough. He was not a pretty feeder, but even then he was memorable.

Conqueror was supreme by virtue of natural genius. The world's heroes are never common clay, and it is difficult to say whether a pack of hounds, any more than a pack of people, really love their masters. Some hounds are a huntsman's solace on a good scent, and some on a bad. Some hounds speak true, and others babble like a party of gossips. Some are great ones for the first two hours and then relapse into skirting or cutting corners, like human folk, and fall into disrepute and ultimate disaster. Conqueror was never led astray by flashy short cuts to the applause of the Field, or a short-timed cheer of a deluded huntsman. He never played to the gallery. What eminent man can lay his hand on his heart and say the same? Nor was he ever jealous that he might be left when, by a stroke of luck, some giftless yapping first-seasoner put up a fox where he had chased a rabbit. Did such an accident of fortune occur, Conqueror would raise his head, wind the breeze and be gone. In a breath of time – were rumour true – his superb mellow note would echo and re-echo through the leaf-carpeted cover, and at once where all had been tension the certainty of pure knowledge was come. From that moment his progress became isolated and spectacular. Word passed rapidly amongst uncouth, strangely mounted farmers, 'Conqueror's gone on.'

Frank Watson, *In the Pink*, 1932

The relationship of the huntsman to his hounds is a personal relationship.

. . . there is no question at all that hounds are affected by the mood their huntsman is in; even his health is known to them – even his personal worries. Supposing the huntsman feels certain that he will not find a fox where he has been asked to draw, it is obvious that he will not have the same enthusiasm as he would where a fox is certain. His doubt is at once picked up by the hounds.

Lord Knutsford in Patrick Chalmers, David James, and Wilson Stephens, *In Praise of Hunting*, 1966

In the later nineteenth century some Masters succumbed to the temptation of breeding hounds for appearance rather than performance in order to win prizes at Peterborough.

'Oh, I am sending a couple of bitches to such and such a dog.'

'Oh, really?' replied his friend. 'Do you know anything about his work?'

'No,' was the reply; 'd—n his work; but he will just correct the little weakness of my bitches below their knees.'

J. Fairfax Blakeborough, Hunting
Reminiscences of H. W. Selby Lowndes, 1926

From my own recollections, I remember my father saying that race-horse breeders would have followed all sorts of foolish breeding fads, if they had not had constantly to submit their animals to the terrible test of the race-course. He was amused that M.F.H.'s had persuaded themselves sometime between the turn of the century and the 1920's, I think, that a foxhound should be forward (or 'over', is it?) at the knee, just as a horse needed to be, to avoid jarring and lameness. A whole generation of English foxhounds was, therefore, bred with forelegs that were either stiffly straight or actually trembling because the knee-joint had been bred to do what no other dog's knee had ever done – curved forward. The Peterborough judges had failed to notice that the canine knee is anatomically the equine fetlock. All the fastest and toughest of dogs – greyhounds or collies – are, of course, way back at the knee and have correspondingly resilient forelegs. I have known a huntsman of those days (Frank Morris of the Cleveland) say that he used to see hounds stumble and actually fall when landing from a jump because their forelegs had been bred to suit this ridiculous showbench requirement. Incidentally, the vogue of 'bone' also came from a mistaken analogy with horses, I believe.

Hon. David Astor in a letter to R. C., 10 December 1974

Horses

Some people have a wonderful pleasure in staring at horses – staring at them just as ladies stare at bonnets.

R. S. Surtees, Mr Facey Romford's
Hounds, 1865

Like the fox and the hound, the horse inspired a spate of anthropomorphic mysticism. The author of the following tribute was an MFH who hunted his hounds.

Oh noble companions, dumb creatures we know,
You lead us in duty and love,
Your honest example in life as you go,
Your courage, devotion and mettle can show
A motive worked out from above.

W. Phillpotts Williams (Master and Huntsman of the
Netton Harriers), The Bonny Grey Mare, 1894

Surtees was too great a novelist to lapse into romantic fallacy.

When a man and his horse differ seriously in public, and the man feels the horse has the best of it, it is wise for the man to appear to accommodate his views to those of the horse, rather than risk a defeat. It is best to let the horse go his way, and pretend it is yours. There is no secret so close as that between a rider and his horse.

R. S. Surtees, Mr Sponge's Sporting Tour, 1853

In Surtees's novels horse-dealers are the nineteenth-century equivalent of second-hand car salesmen. Facey Romford, a representative of the villainous, impoverished, but supremely competent Masters of the hunting under-world, is contemplating buying a horse from Mr Good-heart.

Then the two looked at the strawberry roan. He was, indeed, a fine horse, up to any weight: corky and cheerful looking, but with rather a sinister cast of the eye when anyone approached him.

'Has but one fault,' said Goodheart, complacently; 'has but one fault – kick people over his 'ead as they mount; but easily hobviated,' added he; 'easily hob-viated – strap up a leg as you mount,' producing a strap from his pocket as he spoke.

'Well, but you can't ride him across country on three legs,' observed Romford.

'True,' assented Goodheart. 'True; but then it's only a momentary ebullition of spleen. Soon finds out when he has got his master on his back, and then a child might ride him – ride him with a thread.'

Mr Facey Romford's Hounds, 1865

G. J. Whyte-Melville, a noted philanthropist and the most popular fox-hunting novelist of the Victorian era was himself killed by a fall in 1878.

In the hollow by the pollard, when the crop is tall
    and rank
  Of the dock leaf and the nettle growing free,
Where the bramble and the brushwood straggle
    blindly o'er the bank,
  And the pyat jerks and chatters on the tree.
    There's a fence I never pass
    In the brushwood and the grass,
  But for very shame I turn my head aside,
    While the tears come thick and hot
    And my curse is on the spot –
'Tis the place where the old horse died.

There's his hoof upon the chimney, there's his hide
   upon the chair,
   A better never bent him to the rein;
Now, for all my love and care, I've an empty stall
   and bare;
   I shall never ride my gallant horse again!
      How he laid him out at speed,
      How he loved to have a lead,
   How he snorted in his mettle and his pride!
      Not a flyer of the Hunt
      Was beside him in the front,
   At the place where the old horse died.

Was he blown? I hardly think it. Did he slip? I
   cannot tell.
   We had run for forty minutes in the vale,
He was reaching at his bridle; he was going strong
   and well,
   And he never seemed to falter or to fail;
      Though I sometimes fancy, too,
      That his daring spirit knew
   The task beyond the compass of his stride,
      Yet he faced it true and brave,
      And dropped into his grave,
   At the place where the old horse died.

I was up in half a minute, but he never seemed to stir,
   Though I scored him with my rowels in the fall;
In this life he had not felt before the insult of the
   spur,
   And I knew that it was over once for all.
      When motionless he lay,
      In his cheerless bed of clay,
   Huddled up without an effort on his side –
      'Twas a hard and bitter stroke,
      For his honest back was broke
   At the place where the old horse died.

With a neigh so faint and feeble that it touched me
　　like a groan,
　'Farewell,' he seemed to murmur, 'ere I die;'
Then set his teeth and stretched his limbs, and so I
　　stood alone,
　While the merry chase went heedless sweeping by.
　　Am I womanly and weak
　　If the tear was on my cheek
　For a brotherhood that death can thus divide?
　　If sickened and amazed
　　Through a woeful mist I gazed
　On the place where the old horse died?

There are men both good and wise, who hold that in
　　a future state,
　Dumb creatures we have cherished here below,
Shall give us joyous greeting when we pass the golden
　　gate;
　Is it folly that I hope it may be so?
　　For never man had friend
　　More enduring to the end,
　Truer mate in turn of time and tide.
　　Could I think we'd meet again
　　It would lighten half my pain
　At the place where the old horse died.

The Place where the Old Horse died

A horse bore.

DAUPHIN. I will not change my horse with any that
　treads but on four pasterns. Ça, ha! He bounds from
　the earth as if his entrails were hairs: le cheval
　volant, the Pegasus, qui a les narines de feu! When
　I bestride him, I soar, I am a hawk: he trots the air;
　the earth sings when he touches it; the basest horn
　of his hoof is more musical than the pipe of Hermes.
ORLEANS. He's of the colour of the nutmeg.

DAUPHIN. And of the heat of the ginger. It is a beast for
  Perseus: he is pure air and fire; and the dull elements
  of earth and water never appear in him but only in
  patient stillness while his rider mounts him: he is
  indeed a horse; and all other jades you may call
  beasts.

CONSTABLE. Indeed, my lord, it is a most absolute and
  excellent horse.

DAUPHIN. It is the prince of palfreys; his neigh is like
  the bidding of a monarch and his countenance en-
  forces homage.

ORLEANS. No more, cousin.

DAUPHIN. Nay, the man hath no wit that cannot, from
  the rising of the lark to the lodging of the lamb, vary
  deserved praise on my palfrey: it is a theme as fluent
  as the sea; turn the sands into eloquent tongues, and
  my horse is argument for them all. 'Tis a subject for
  a sovereign to reason on, and for a sovereign's sovereign to ride on; and for the world – familiar to us,
  and unknown – to lay apart their particular functions
  and wonder at him. I once writ a sonnet in his praise
  and began thus: 'Wonder of nature!'

William Shakespeare, *Henry V*, 1623

Masters

'If I had Mr Darcy's money, I would keep a pack of hounds.'

Master Lucas in Jane Austen, *Pride and Prejudice*, 1813

Above all Puff felt that he was a new man in the country, and that taking the hounds would give him weight.

Mr Puffington on the prospect of becoming an MFH.
R. S. Surtees, *Mr Sponge's Sporting Tour*, 1853

Surtees's great creation John Jorrocks was a Cockney grocer. An unlikely MFH, he addresses his hunt in his famous 'lector'.

'Of all sitivations under the sun, none is more enviable or more 'onerable than that of a master of fox 'ounds! Talk of a M.P.! vot's an M.P. compared to an M.F.H.? Your M.P. lives in a tainted hatmosphere among other M.P.'s and loses his consequences by the commonness of the office, and the scoldings he gets from those who sent him there, but an M.F.H. holds his levee in the stable, his levee in the kennel, and his levee in the 'untin' field – is great and important every where – has no one to compete with him, no one to find fault, but all join in doing honour to him to whom honour is so greatly due (cheers). And oh, John Jorrocks! my good frind,' continued the worthy grocer, fumbling the silver in his small clothes with upturned eyes to heaven, 'to think that you, after all the hups and downs of life – the crossin's and jostlin's of merchandise and ungovernable trade – the sortin' of sugars – the mexin' of teas – the postin' of ledgers, and handlin' of inwoices, to think that you, my dear feller, should have arrived at this distinguished post is most miraculously wonderful, most singularly queer. Gentlemen, *this* is the proudest moment of my life! (cheers). I've now reached the top-rail in the ladder of my hambition! (renewed cheers).'

Handley Cross, 1843

By a literary and musical accident a Cumberland yeoman, John Peel, has become the most famous of all Masters. For half a century (he died in 1854) he kept hounds on £400 a year.

A description of Peel in 1829 was that he wore corduroy knee trousers and ankle-jacks, a very strong tall silk hat as worn in those days, which got pretty well weathered and battered with the gales and rough work of the hunting field, and he carried his whip and twined horn in his right hand as shown in photographs.

I presume he only had one hat, or that any other got equally dilapidated. 'Dunny,' his horse, is said to have come out of the pot cart of a hawker called Peter Flynch, and used to follow him like a dog whenever the rough country made it impossible to ride, as frequently happened. Dunny stood about 14.3, was tough as nails, with fairly deep shoulders and a very strong loin. He was trained to wait indefinitely for either father or son and to kneel for his mount if required. . . . Peel was clever at cutting corners to get on even terms with his hounds or fox, yet if a straight run was wanted, he had plenty of latent energy, and nothing would stop him. After a hunt, he would occasionally exercise his lungs with a few holloas on the way home, so that not only did his horn wake the natives in the morning, but his voice sometimes kept them from sleep in the evening, if his return was late.

Hugh Machell, *John Peel*, 1926

For Trollope Lord Chiltern embodied the virtues of the ideal Master.

It is essential that a Master of Hounds should be somewhat feared by the men who ride with him. There should be much awe mixed with the love felt for him. He should be a man with whom other men will not care to argue; an irrational, cut and thrust, unscrupulous, but yet distinctly honest man; one who can be tyrannical, but will tyrannise only over the evil spirits; a man capable of intense cruelty to those alongside of him, but who will know whether his victim does in truth deserve scalping before he draws his knife. He should be savage and yet good-humoured; severe and yet forbearing; truculent and pleasant in the same moment. He should exercise unflinching authority, but should do so with the consciousness that he can support it only by his own popularity. His speech should be short, incisive, always to the point, but never founded on argument. His rules are based on no reason, and will never bear discussion. He must be the most candid of men, also the most close; – and yet never a hypocrite. He must condescend to no explanation, and

yet must impress men with an assurance that his de-
cisions will certainly be right. He must rule all as
though no man's special welfare were of any account,
and yet must administer all so as to offend none.
Friends he must have, but not favourites. He must be
self-sacrificing, diligent, eager, and watchful. He must
be strong in health, strong in heart, strong in purpose,
and strong in purse. He must be economical and yet
lavish; generous as the wind and yet obdurate as the
frost. He should be assured that of all human pursuits
hunting is the best, and that of all living things a fox is
the most valuable. He must so train his heart as to feel
for the fox a mingled tenderness and cruelty which is
inexplicable to ordinary men and women. His desire to
preserve the brute and then to kill him should be
equally intense and passionate. And he should do it all
in accordance with a code of unwritten laws, which
cannot be learnt without profound study.

Lord Chiltern on a bad day.

At one o'clock they had not found, and the hilarity of
the really hunting men as they ate their sandwiches and
lit their cigars was on the decrease. The ladies talked
more than ever, Lady Gertrude's voice was heard above
them all, and Lord Chiltern trotted on close behind his
hounds in obdurate silence. When things were going
bad with him no one in the field dared to speak to him.

Anthony Trollope, *Phineas Redux*, 1874

Regency Masters were often Regency Rakes.

John Chaworth Musters (1777–1849) – always known
as Jack Musters – was a far better huntsman than
Mytton but scarcely a better man. Son of a great
beauty, he was exceedingly handsome; vain, he became
a compulsive womanizer. 'Handsome Jack,' as his

biographer puts it, 'unfortunately had an ineradicable propensity to make love to every woman he met.' In 1805 he married a rich heiress, Mary Chaworth. Even Byron, whose first love she was, might have made a more satisfactory husband than Musters, whose infidelity finally affected his wife's mind. Like many of his sort he was popular with men, who valued his skill as a breeder of hounds and horses (he sold his favourite hunter for 500 guineas in 1800), his superb horsemanship and his 'manliness'. He fought Assheton Smith at Eton till their faces were pulp, and later all members of the 'lower orders' who offended him. He was as appallingly rude in the field as he was 'delightful' in the drawing-room; to a lame parson who overrode hounds he shouted, 'There goes that damned parson. He's as deformed in mind as he is in body.' He ended his days hunting any subscription pack that would have him. Yet in his great days as master of the Pytchley he was 'the king of gentlemen huntsmen' and he made a not inconsiderable contribution to the speeding up of the sport. Meynell considered Musters his best pupil. 'To Mr Musters,' wrote Nimrod, 'as a huntsman, the sporting world have unhesitatingly assigned the palm of superiority.'

An even less respectable representative of the moral code of some Regency masters was Squire George Forester of Willey, whose whipper-in was the immortal Tom Moody. Forester's twin passions were fox hunting and womanizing. For the one he rose at 4 am to dine at 3 pm, leaving him, early in the day, free to pursue the other. He kept his mistresses (to his credit they were chosen for their horsemanship) openly in 'his' village, building a raised pavement beside his carriage drive so that they might keep their feet dry walking to the big house. The most celebrated was Miss Phoebe Higgs, probably the most reckless horsewoman who ever rode to hounds. She would jump seemingly impossible places and challenge the Squire and Tom Moody to follow her. On one occasion she confronted the Squire with a loaded pistol, and threatened to shoot him if he did not give her a bigger allowance than he was giving one of her rivals. She spent her free days visiting the poor. Forester had Mytton's love of horse-play at the cost of dependants who could not retaliate. His parson, almost permanently occupied in christening the Squire's bastards, once stole hungry to the larder in the middle of the night in search of a slice of venison; the Squire heard him and, turning the larder-door key, later released the poor man and a bag fox at the same time. The fox chased the parson in his nightshirt round the house. Worst of all, perhaps, he enjoyed making Moody drunk with bumpers of port out of a fox's mask and then expected him to ride well next day. Not that Moody needed encouragement. Stephen Goodall, first of the great Goodall dynasty of huntsmen, had whipped-in to Moody and, as a fine huntsman himself, could not understand Moody's professional reputation. 'He was fonder of fishing than hunting and liked strong ale better than either.' He probably made up his exploits in the ale house whence they entered into the ever-receptive verse (and it is terrible verse at that) mythology of hunting heroes, just as his death was immortalized by a series of sporting prints.

Raymond Carr, *English Foxhunting*, 1976

Fashionable packs attracted Masters who cared little for fox-hunting. The Marquis of Hastings was a disaster for the Quorn in 1866; his hangovers were so tremendous that he could not blow his horn for fear of being sick in front of his field.

When will the Marquis come? Who can tell?
Half past twelve or half past one – who can tell?
Is he sober, is he drunk nipping like Mynheer Van
    Dunk
Will he ride or will he funk? Who can tell?

Anon., quoted in C. V. B. Ellis, *Leicestershire and The Quorn Hunt*, 1951

Lord Suffield was short of cash when his horse was beaten by a 'cripple' in the Derby.

His stud groom reported that dealers would no longer supply corn for the hunt horses on credit. 'Get hay from the farmers' was the master's reply. 'No good, my lord, they won't send a thing either; in fact the pastry cook is the only tradesman who will take an order.' 'Then for God's sake feed them on pastry.' By 1840 he had to resign. He had bought Mr Ralph Lambton's pack for £3,000; he now sold it back to the north for £1,000 and the Quorn were left with no master and no hounds.

Raymond Carr, *English Foxhunting*, 1976

Lord Wilton, the last of the 'Kings of Melton' and the finest rider of his day was of a different mould.

Whilst on his switch-tailed bay, with wandering eye
Attenuated Wilton canters by.
His character, how difficult to know
A compound of psalm tunes and Tally-ho!
A forward rider, half inclined to preach
Though not disposed to practise or to teach
An amorous lover with a saintly twist
And now a jockey and now an organist.

The Chaunt of Achilles (supposed to have been written by Mr Ralph Bernal Osborne)

*Thomas Assheton Smith, Master of his own pack, the
Tedworth 1826–58, was an austere autocrat who dis-
approved of drinking and gambling. Greatly praised for
restoring respectability to the hunting field, two thousand
riders turned out to celebrate his return to the Quorn
country in 1840. His huntsman, George Carter (b. 1792)
took a less enthusiastic view of his qualities as a Master.*

Oh dear, dear me, and he were an odd man, a very
odd man were Mr Smith; why, he were unlike any one
else, and didn't care what he did or what he said. Why
there, he used in frosty weather, when he couldn't go
a-hunting, to have down three or four horses to the
ride, and he'd make me, or Lees, or some one else, stay
there, and he'd gallop round and round, as hard as
ever he could and just in the same track, and I don't
believe he would have pulled up if any one had been in
his way. 'Twere just the same going home from hunting, hard as ever he could gallop, when he didn't have
his carriage you know, sir. Why I've been going along
quiet with the hounds towards Sidbury Hill, coming
back from Everley that way, and I've seen Mr Smith
coming along galloping and waving his hand, and I've
said to Cowley, 'We must get out o' the way, or Mr
Smith will be right over us;' and he never turned either
way, but by he went, and never took any notice of us
or hound, or anything else. Of course you know, sir, I
put my hand up to my cap as he passed, and so did
Cowley. Oh, he were a very odd man! Why, sir, I've
know'd him of a Sunday wait at the church door after
the service, and I'd try not to see him, for I know'd
what would happen; and there he'd stand till I come
up, and then I'd hear, 'George,' 'Carter' (for I didn't
seem to hear him, you know sir, the first time); and I'd
come up and say, 'I beg your pardon, sir, but did you
wish to speak to me?' And then he'd begin asking what

hounds I was a going to take out the next day, and all about the hunting, sir, and there were the people, you know, all stopt back, as couldn't get out of church; and I'd say, 'I beg your pardon, sir, but hadn't I better come down to the House, sir, and see you, sir, and then you can tell me what you like; for these good people, you see, sir, want to get out of church, sir.' And then he'd say, 'Oh! do they? Well, I suppose they do; well, you come down.' And then on he'd go, but he never thought anything of it, and that too of a Sunday and coming out o' church. Oh! I was quite ashamed of him.

The Life and Recollections of George Carter, the Great
Huntsman, 1885

The irascible Master is a stock character. Mr Sponge, the itinerant fox-hunter, is reproved by Lord Scamperdale. His huntsman is Jack Spraggon.

The day, too, seemed changing for the worse; a heavy black cloud hanging overhead. The hounds were at length brought to their noses.

His lordship, who had been riding all eyes, ears, and fears, foresaw the probability of this; and pulling-to his horse, held up his hand, the usual signal for Jack to 'sing out' and stop the field. Sponge saw the signal, but, unfortunately, Hercules didn't; and tearing along with his head to the ground, resolutely bore our friend not only past his lordship, but right on to where the now stooping pack were barely feathering on the line.

Then Jack and his lordship sung out together.

'*Hold hard!*' screeched his lordship, in a dreadful state of excitement.

'HOLD HARD!' thundered Jack.

Sponge *was* holding hard – hard enough to split the horse's jaws, but the beast would go on, notwithstanding.

'By the powers, he's among 'em again!' shouted his lordship, as the resolute beast, with his upturned head almost pulled round to Sponge's knee, went stargazing on like the blind man in Regent Street. '*Sing out*, Jack! sing out! for heaven's sake sing out,' shrieked his lordship, shutting his eyes, as he added, 'or he'll kill every man Jack of them.'

'Now, SUR!' roared Jack, 'can't you steer that ere aggravatin' quadruped of yours?'

'Oh, you pestilential son of a pontry-maid!' screeched his lordship, as Brilliant ran yelping away from under Sponge's horse's feet. '*Sing out Jack! sing out!*' gasped his lordship again.

'Oh, you scandalous, hypocritical, rusty-booted, numb-handed son of a puffing corn-cutter, why don't you turn your attention to feeding hens, cultivating cabbages, or making pantaloons for small folks, instead of killing hounds in this wholesale way?' roared Jack; an enquiry that set him foaming again.

'Oh, you unsighty, sanctified, idolatrous, Bagnigge-Wells coppersmith, you think because I'm a lord, and can't swear or use coarse language, that you may do what you like; rot you, sir, I'll present you with a testimonial! I'll settle a hundred a-year upon you if you'll quit the country. *By the powers*, they're away again!' added his lordship.

R. S. Surtees, *Mr Sponge's Sporting Tour*, 1853

A chestnut retailed by Nimrod.

A well-mounted man had one day been pressing so closely on his hounds, that nothing but a Job could stand it any longer, and Mr Nicoll bestowed upon him a few hearty damns. The offender rode up to him and said, 'Upon my word, Mr Nicoll, I don't understand this, Sir! I did not *come out* to be damn'd' – 'Then go home and be damn'd!' replied Mr Nicoll.

Nimrod, *Hunting Tours*, 1835

Anthony Powell's Mr Passenger is in the tradition of irascible MFHs. He is talking to his daughter at the meet.

'Here's the Master,' said Jasper, and swept off his hat, releasing his ears from under it so that they flew out on either side of his head in their accustomed high relief.

Mr Passenger certainly seemed to be in a bad temper. He was red in the face and was riding his heavily built chestnut with a short rein and giving a series of nods and grunts while he listened to Captain Hudgins-Coot, the hunt secretary, who was riding beside him and who was evidently trying to explain away some appalling fiasco that had taken place. . . .

'Hullo, Father. You're looking younger than ever this morning. What's made you so pleased?'

Mr Passenger said: 'I've just caught that damned nursery-maid of yours trying to offer Affable a sandwich. If that sort of thing happens again I warn you she will have to go. I won't have her in the house. I'll turn her out bag and baggage.'

Betty said: 'Who on earth is Affable? The new footman? Don't tell me she has fallen for him, Father. I simply don't believe it. He's got spots.'

Mr Passenger looked with attention at his elder daughter for several seconds. He appeared to be contemplating something really stinging in the way of a reply but for some reason he thought better of it and merely said:

'Affable is the soundest hound in the pack. I might almost say the only sound hound in the pack. Anyway, the incident has some importance as creating a precedent, so I hope you will impress Whatshername with the gravity of her attempted act.'

From a View to a Death, 1933

Lord Leconfield was Master of his own hounds. His nephew describes a solitary hunt in wartime.

We found a fox and lost it, and while Uncle Charles' huntsman was casting for it we heard a tremendous hullabaloo about two miles away. Uncle Charles abused the huntsman and shouted at him, 'Can't you hear a holler?' and bade him 'Get going thither'. So we galloped in the direction of the noise, only to find it had nothing to do with fox hunting: it was a village football match. The hounds, the huntsman, the whipper-in, Uncle Charles and I all slithered to a stop. There was silence, then Uncle Charles, who had turned red in the face, stood up in his stirrups and shouted: 'Haven't you people got anything better to do in war time than play *football*?' We then went on hunting.

John Wyndham, *Wyndham and Children First*, 1968

Hunt Servants

I have always thought a huntsman a happy man: his office is pleasing, and at the same time flattering: we pay him for that which diverts him, and he is enriched by his greatest pleasure; nor is a general, after a victory, more proud than is a huntsman who returns with his fox's head.

Peter Beckford, *Thoughts on Hunting*, 1781

It is easier to find a good Prime Minister than a good huntsman.

Lord Chaplin (1840–1923),
Minister of Education
and Master of the Blankney

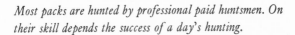

Most packs are hunted by professional paid huntsmen. On their skill depends the success of a day's hunting.

You can tell an experienced huntsman at once, because he is about an eighth of a second quicker than the pack in saying the word 'Go.' After which it is his duty to amuse the Field by his language – a purely technical expression for those traditional admonitions and exhortations, mostly of French patois origin, which every intelligent hound naturally understands. While the pack are drawing a huntsman will touch his horn to show the Field he is still all there, by which I mean, of course, still in the cover, and in a high cracked voice permit himself reflections all nicely joined up companionable-like, as 'eleuin,' 'edawickedawick' (crack), 'yoiwindimthur' (horn), 'yoirouseimmelads' and 'loointhur.' Hounds in the meantime are too busy for such transports, and presently when one 'challenges,' as the old books called it, the huntsman will show even more medieval learning, and crying 'Hoicktogether,' or 'Forridhoick,' will proceed with a noise like a hen laying an egg. When you hear that make straight for the nearest gate, because it is quite on the cards there will follow that paralysing call to action, 'Taa-leo awawoy!' when everyone with frenzied leisure permits an ambitious dealer to take the heart out of the nearest fence.

Frederick Watson, *Hunting Pie*, 1931

A huntsman that I once knew (who, by the bye, I believe, is at this time a drummer in a marching regiment) went out one morning so very drunk, that he got off his horse in the midst of a thick cover, laid himself down, and went to sleep: he was lost; nobody knew what was become of him; and he was at last found in the situation that I have just described. He had, however, great good luck on his side; for, at the very instant he was found, a fox was halloo'd; upon which he mounted his horse, rode desperately, killed his fox handsomely, and was forgiven.

Peter Beckford, *Thoughts on Hunting*, 1781

Lord Henry Bentinck, reformer of racing and himself one of the greatest breeders of hounds, describes the practice of Will Goodall, huntsman of the Belvoir 1842–59. Goodall's skills as a breeder had a profound influence on the blood of English foxhounds.

Goodall's chief aim was to get the hearts of his Hounds. He considered Hounds should be treated like women; that they would not bear to be bullied, to be deceived, or neglected with impunity. For this end, he would not meddle with them in their casts until they had done trying for themselves, and felt the want of him; he paid them the compliment of going to fetch them; he never

[32]

deceived or neglected them; he was continually cheering and making much of the Hounds; and if he was
compelled to disappoint them by roughly stopping
them off a suckling vixen or dying Fox at dark, you
would see him as soon as he had got them stopped,
jump off his horse, get into the middle of the pack, and
spend ten minutes in making friends with them again.
The result was that the Hounds were never happy
without him, and when lost would drive up through
any crowd of horsemen to get to him again, and it was
very rare for a single Hound to be left out.

Goodall's Practice, 1846

From the cradle his name has been 'Hard-riding Dick'
Since the time when cock-horse he bestraddled a stick;
Since the time when, unbreech'd, without saddle or
    rein,
He kick'd the old jackass along the green lane.

Dick, wasting no time o'er the classical page,
Spent his youth in the stable without any wage;
The life of poor Dick when he enter'd his 'teens,
Was to sleep in the hayloft and breakfast on beans.

Promoted at length, Dick's adventures began: –
A stripling on foot, but when mounted a man;
Capp'd, booted, and spurr'd, his young soul was on
    fire,
The day he was dubb'd 'Second Whip' to the Squire.

*   *   *

A whip is Dick's sceptre, a saddle Dick's throne,
And a horse is the kingdom he rules as his own;
While grasping ambition encircles the earth,
The dominions of Dick are enclosed in a girth.

Three ribs hath he broken, two legs, and one arm,
But there hangs, it is said, round his neck a life-charm;
Still, long odds are offer'd that Dick, when he drops,
Will die, as he lived, in his breeches and tops.

> R. E. Egerton Warburton,
> 'Hard-riding Dick' from *Hunting Songs*, 1877

Parson brought 'is Bible and come to read to me.
' 'Ave what you like, there's everything within this
    Book,' says he.
Says I, 'They've left the 'orses out.' Says 'e, 'You are
    mistook;'
An' 'e up an' read a 'eap of things about them from
    the Book.

> Sir Arthur Conan Doyle, 'The Dying Whip' from *The
> Poems of Arthur Conan Doyle*, 1922

The Field

Masters frequently debate, in their secret conclaves, whether there is any way of abolishing the Field. They are confident that hunting would be removed above carping criticism if no one hunted.

*   *   *

Old huntsmen never quite lose the habit of peering over the left shoulder. Is it memories of the Master's languishing eye? No, sir, it is not. Is it because a couple of hounds are missing? It'll learn 'em to catch up. Is it for a Christmas Box? Certainly not. No. A huntsman is haunted – forever haunted – by the menacing thunder of the galloping field.

Frederick Watson, *Hunting Pie*, 1931

The country Squires' devotion to the chase was scorned by the men of fashion.

MR WILDISH. A man must be wak'd at three in a Morning, by the crack'd voices of Huntsmen, with damn'd Bugle-Horns, and the confounded yelps of Curs: and for want of Friendship with Men, divert themselves with their Enmity to Beasts; and hunt, as if the Devil were in 'em, till at dark Night they are scarce able to dismount their Horses.

Ld BELLAMY. They are Fops, *Ned*, that make a Business of Sport. I hunt with my Harriers half a dozen Heats in a Morning for Health and an Appetite: and at Dinner time, let 'em be in never such full cry, I knock off.

WILDISH. There is some Reason in that; but your true Country 'Squire lives in Boots all the Winter, never talks of anything but Sports as he calls 'em: and if an ill Day comes, saunters about his House, lolls upon Couches; sighs and groans, as if he were a Prisoner in the *Fleet*; and the best thing he can find to do, is to Smoak, and Drink, and play at Backgammon, with the Parson.

BELLAMY. These are of the strictest order of Hunters, such as keep Journals of every Day's hunting, and write long Letters of Fox-chases from one end of England to the other. Tho' these are Fops, *Ned*, a Reasonable Man may enjoy himself very well in the country.

Thomas Shadwell, Bury Fair, 1689

A shaft of humour breaks through the arid Journal of the Althorp Hunt, kept by Lady Spencer after dinner :

23 March: Mr Bouverie had a fall but was not hurt.

I wish to God he had been [*scribbled in the margin by another hand*].

G. Paget, The History of the Althorp and Pytchley, 1937

Sir Roger de Coverley was a fox-hunting squire in his youth.

His stable Doors are patched with Noses that belonged to Foxes of the Knight's own hunting down. Sir Roger showed me one of them that for Distinction sake has a Brass Nail struck through it, which cost him about fifteen Hours riding, carried him through half a Dozen Counties, killed him a Brace of Geldings, and lost above half his Dogs. This the Knight looks upon as one of the greatest Exploits of his Life. The perverse Widow, whom I have given some Account of, was the

Death of several foxes; for Sir Roger has told me that in the Course of his Amours he patched the Western Door of his Stable. Whenever the Widow was cruel, the Foxes were sure to pay for it. In proportion as his Passion for the Widow abated and old Age came on, he left off Fox-hunting; but a Hare is not yet safe that sits within ten Miles of his House.

Spectator, 1711–12

In the late eighteenth century fox-hunting expanded beyond the Squire and his friends. Dr Johnson and Beau Brummell tried it.

He certainly rode on Mr Thrale's old hunter with a good grimness, and though he would follow the hounds fifty miles on end sometimes, would never own himself either tired or amused. 'I have now learned,' said he, 'by hunting, to perceive that it is no diversion at all, nor ever takes a man out of himself for a moment: the dogs have less sagacity than I could have prevailed on myself to suppose; and the gentlemen often call to me not to ride over them. It is very strange and very melancholy, that the paucity of human pleasures should persuade us ever to call hunting one of them.' He was, however, proud to be amongst the sportsmen; and I think no praise ever went so close to his heart, as when Mr Hamilton called out one day upon Brighthelmstone Downs, 'Why, Johnson rides as well, for aught I see, as the most illiterate fellow in England.'

Mrs Thrale, *Anecdotes of
the late Samuel Johnson*, 1788

Beau Brummell, God bless us, how ventures he here,
    Delighting our eyes and our noses?
He splashes through ditches, in kerseymere breeches,
    All streaming with attar of roses.

Anon.

*   *   *

Though Brummell was so much at Belvoir, and kept a stud of horses there, he was never a 'Melton man'; and his friends, as well as everyone else, were amazingly astonished when he joined in the pleasures of the chase; for, like many other gentlemen, he did not like it: it did not suit his habits, and his servant could never get him up in time to join the hounds, if it was a distant meet: but even if the meet was near, and they found quickly, he only rode a few fields, and then shaped his course in an opposite direction, or paid a visit to the nearest farm-house, to satisfy his enormous appetite for bread and cheese. I have heard him, but many years after, laugh amazingly over these incidents of his Melton days, and say in his usual droll way, that he 'could not bear to have his tops and leathers splashed by the greasy galloping farmers.'

Attributed to Captain Jesse, 1778–1840
From *A Foxhunter's Anthology*, ed. Peter Lewis, 1934

Henry Green the novelist (1905–73) hunted as a boy with the Ledbury. It was taken for granted that he would do so; but his heart was not in it and his hunting career was brief.

All I remember of those days is the excessive cordiality my elders used towards each other at the meet, the terror with which most of them waited while the covert

was drawn, and the excessive rudeness which came
over them in that first gallop there is after the hounds
have found after which I would be left. Chipping, the
groom, and I would make our way diagonally across
the circles foxes usually make their way by; if you know
where the coverts are and what they call the line foxes
take then by diligently trotting, with time to spare to
shut open gates, you come upon the field quite often
and then as likely as not be in danger of heading the
hunted fox. My Mother's father I believe went out
with a servant who carried two axes in his saddle and
because there was so much wire in his country (they
were his own hounds) every variety of wire clipper as
well and yet he saw as much as anyone of what went on.
Those who, galloping hard and jumping everything,
were seldom out of sight of hounds were seldom out of
earshot of his voice encouraging his man as he chopped
the fences down, for my grandfather had lost his nerve
and would not jump. After hunting so they say he
would go out in his pink coat, still in his boots and play
golf in the park with his butler in a bowler hat carrying
the clubs.

Pack My Bag, 1940

*Most fox-hunters believed that the spread of railway lines
would make fox-hunting impossible by transforming 'the
rural soil into one vast gridiron'. Surtees, the realist, saw
that railways could only increase the popularity and
availability of the sport. It was the 'railway revolution'
that allowed Londoners like John Jorrocks to hunt beyond
the suburbs of London.*

When the gates of the world were opened by railways,
our friend's active mind saw that business might be
combined with pleasure, and as first one line opened
and then another, he shot down into the different
countries – bags and all – Beckford in one pocket –

order book in the other – hunting one day and selling teas another. Nay, he sometimes did both together, and they tell a story of him in Wiltshire, holloaing out to a man who had taken a fence to get rid of him, 'Did you say *two* chests o' black and *one* o' green?' Then when the Great Northern opened he took a turn down to Peterborough, and emboldened by what he saw with Lord Fitzwilliam, he at length ventured, right into the heaven of heavens – the grass – or what he calls the 'cut 'em down' countries. What a commotion he caused! Which is Jorrocks? Show me Jorrocks! Is that old Jorrocks! and men would ride to and fro eyeing him as if he were a wild beast.

R. S. Surtees, *Handley Cross*, 1843

It was the sheer excitements of Midland Hunting that brought crowds to Leicestershire. The most famous run in the history of fox-hunting was the Billesdon Coplow (24 February 1800); it lasted two and a quarter hours over twenty-eight miles.

The Coplow of Billesdon, ne'er witnessed I ween
Two hundred such horses and men, at a burst
All determined to ride – each resolved to be first . . .

These excitements posed problems as fields grew larger.

Do we ever see runs like those of old in the present day? If not, what is the cause? Hounds never were better than now, or altogether better managed. The sole reason is this: where in former days there were fifty men out there are now three hundred. Formerly five or six men used to ride hard, and if they knew but little of hunting, they generally knew when hounds were on scent and when not. At present everybody rides hard, and out of three hundred, not three have the slightest notion whether they are on or off scent. Although probably there are not three horses which could live with them through a clipping run, there are an ample number good enough to ride over them, and prevent their settling to a scent. When hounds are up to the mark they are apt to have a little fling and fly in them, and to go over it, and if they have room will come back again and catch hold of it; but how is it possible with three hundred red-coats close to their sterns? When there is a lack of sport one man abuses the hounds, another the huntsman . . . It is difficult to know what to do with an immense ungovernable field. If you do not cast your hounds the steam of the horses and the noise of the crowd will prevent their hunting through it, and if you do cast them too much they are always looking for the huntsman. If therefore there is want of sport, let people attribute it to the right cause, which is the jealousy and *ignorance of the sportsmen*, and not the badness of the hounds, or want of science in the huntsman. If hounds were let alone and not ridden upon, they could rarely miss a day's sport.

Sir Charles Knightley, Master of the Pytchley (1809–17) in W. Scarth Dixon, *History of the Bramham Moor Hunt*, 1899

Fox-hunters of the old school and ageing addicts could not keep up with the new pace.

Another of the old school of sportsmen whose going days were over just as I appeared on the scene in Leicestershire was Mr Gaskin, who lived at Sysonby Lodge, a hunting-box on the Kettleby and Melton road. The old gentleman knew every yard of the country with gates and gaps, so that he could trot about and get a bird's-eye view of all that was going on. With him rode a second horseman armed with a hatchet and saw; and directly they came to a fence that had been mended up, he would say, 'John, here is one of our gaps made up. Clear it all out, clear it all out at once!'

Instead of a hunting-crop he carried a thick walking-stick, and if his horse would not stand still while his servant was reducing the fence, he would crash it down on his head, shouting, 'Whoa, won't you stand still!' In his younger days it was said he went well to hounds, thoroughly enjoying the ride, but when he was reduced to trotting about to look at the rising generation negotiating a strongly-fenced country, he would set his teeth and grin with delight, exclaiming, 'Look at the lunatics, John! Look at them!'

Reminiscences of Frank Gillard, Huntsman
with the Belvoir 1860–96

The phrase 'painting the town (Melton) red' comes from the activities of Regency Bucks after a day's hunting. Lady Augusta Fane describes a later exploit.

We found Melton as usual, crammed with hunting people. Sir Beaumont and Lady Florence Dixie had the 'Old Club'; she kept a jaguar in the garden to the great alarm of the parson who lived next door. The three brothers Flower (Horace, Herbert and Peter) were at North Lodge; and it was there that Peter Flower made a bet, during dinner, that he would ride a horse up the stairs to the first floor. One of his hunters was promptly saddled and led into the Hall. Peter leapt on his back and galloped up the stairs on to the landing, but once there nothing would induce the animal to come down again. All this happened on a Saturday night, so upstairs the horse had to remain till Monday morning, when he was lowered out of the window by means of a hastily constructed platform and ropes. Lord Annaly subsequently bought the horse and named him 'First Flight'.

Chit Chat, 1926

By the later nineteenth century, Lady Augusta Fane was one of the dashing women who hunted regularly in the Shires. To liberators of women – often 'antis' – it must come as a surprise that fox-hunting was the first sport open to women. The poetic objections to women hunting were put forward by James Thomson in 1730.

But if the rougher sex by this fierce sport
Is hurried wild, let not such horrid joy
E'er stain the bosom of the British fair.
Far be the spirit of the chase from them!
Uncomely courage, unbeseeming skill,
To spring the fence, to reign the prancing steed,
The cap, the whip, the masculine attire
In which they roughen to the sense and all
The winning softness of their sex is lost.
In them 'tis graceful to dissolve at woe;
With every motion, every word, to wave
Quick o'er the kindling cheek the ready blush;
And from the smallest violence to shrink.

The Seasons, 1730

Gradually the objections weakened.

When women do ride they generally ride like the very devil. There is no medium with them. They either 'go' to beat the men, or they don't 'go' at all. We have seen

[43]

some uncommon performers among women, performers that would put nine-tenths of the men to the blush. We are puzzled whether to give the palm to the single or to the married women in this respect; but, as the single are most interesting, perhaps the preference will be yielded to them. Like many things in this world it makes all the difference who the party is that hunts. If a pretty woman hunts we are all glad to see her; if an ugly one comes we wonder what 'brings her out.' Certainly dishevelled hair, ruddy and perspiring face, and muddy habit, are more likely to be forgiven in the bloom of youth than in what ought to be the orderly sobriety of maturer years. We had dotted down a lot of names of first-rate female performers across country, but in looking it over we find it contains such a curious medley, that we think it better to suppress it altogether than risk the chance of offending by publishing an unpalatable assortment.

Never having been a woman, we cannot understand how it is they manage to keep their seats. We see what are called 'washball' seated men rolling about constantly, and yet women, to whom the term as well as the form is much more applicable and becoming, manage to keep on. Keeping their seats on the road, and keeping them in the field are very different things, about as different as riding horses on the road and riding them with hounds. 'Still, where there's a will there's a way,' and pretty dears who would scream at the sight of a frog or a mouse, will face a bullfinch from which many men would turn away – indeed that is one of the palpable inconveniences of ladies hunting, for it is almost a point of honour for men to go over what ladies have taken. If it were not their ignorance when horses have done enough, and their great desire for pace, we would rather be a woman's horse than a man's. Women have much finer, and more delicate hands than men, and they never fight or bully their horses as men do – neither do they ever pull them into their leaps – by which means nine-tenths of the annual falls are procured.

R. S. Surtees, *Analysis of the Hunting Field*, 1846

Conservative Masters like Surtees's Lord Ladythorne did not welcome women.

'They say she's the finest oss-woman that ever was seen.'

'Indeed' mused his lordship, thinking over the pros and cons of female equestrianism – the disagreeableness of being beat by them – the disagreeableness of having to leave them in the lurch – the disagreeableness of seeing them floored – the disagreeableness of seeing them all running down with perspiration; – the result being that his lordship adhered to his established opinion that women have no business out hunting.

R. S. Surtees, *Ask Mamma*, 1858

Catherine Walters, 'Skittles,' the poule de luxe, *who for a time became W. S. Blunt's mistress, was a keen follower of hounds.*

I have been told that 'Skittles' was the last of the great 'demi-mondaines' of the 'sixties, and that she was a well-educated, clever woman, devoted to riding and hunting. She went to Melton Mowbray with Lord Hopetoun to hunt with the Quorn when Lord Stamford was MFH. Now Lady Stamford, his second wife, was reported to have come from the same social set as 'Skittles' and to have started life as one of the three handsome daughters of a Norfolk keeper. This tale may be true or not, but anyhow Lady Stamford objected to a rival in the hunting field, so she sent for her lord and master and insisted that he should 'dispatch that improper woman home,' declaring that it was a scandal that so notorious a person should dare to hunt with the Quorn Hounds.

On being told of this discussion by a friend, 'Skittles' at once turned her horse for Melton, being too keen a sportswoman to wish to make trouble in the hunting field and embarrass the MFH. As good luck would have it, before she had gone far, a fox crossed the road in front of her, followed by the hounds in full cry. This was too much for 'Skittles'; she jumped the fence and joined in the chase and rode so straight and well that at the end of the run Lord Stamford congratulated her, and swore she must always hunt with the Quorn 'and damn all jealous women.' To show her displeasure Lady Stamford never went to another meet whilst her husband was master.

'Skittles' was reported to be very strict with her lovers, and during the hunting season they had to be contented with love at a distance, as she said that hunting and love could not be allowed to interfere with each other.

Lady Augusta Fane, *Chit Chat*, 1926

In 1876 the Empress of Austria began her regular visits to hunt in England. She succeeded the now middle-aged Catherine Walters as the most famous female follower of hounds.

The Empress had the *entrée* into every fashionable gathering in London or in Leicestershire, and her feats in the saddle became legendary, just as Catherine's had become legendary a decade previously. She had also taken a leaf out of Catherine's book by appearing at dinner parties at Easton Neston wearing the very simplest of evening dresses, usually in black or ivory velvet, and almost without jewellery, but with the folds clinging seductively to the outlines of her figure. And like Catherine she could neither think nor talk about anything else than horses and hunting whilst she was in England. Hunting came before love-making, and hunting came even before accepting royal commands from Windsor to visit the Queen for luncheon.

In dress and figure she was very reminiscent of Catherine in her hey-day. She, too, used to have her riding clothes tailored so closely to her figure that every contour was revealed, and she, too, was often sewn naked into her habit before she went out hunting.

Henry Blythe, *Skittles*, 1970

Margot Asquith was the wife of the Liberal Prime Minister, Henry Asquith.

Before she married, Margot Asquith hunted regularly in Leicestershire, and rode with the same vigour aud energy that she throws into all her actions. She was not a particularly good horse-woman, but she had plenty of pluck, and had to be in the 'first flight' or die in the attempt!

In some walks of life men are supposed to 'follow their leaders,' but most certainly in the hunting field 'women lead their followers,' and there were many young 'bloods' who pursued Margot over the fences, only to be told by their enchantress that they 'looked like a string of onions trailing after her!' After Margot married she was selling some of her horses, and I asked her the name of a useful-looking hunter she was riding, to which she replied: 'I call him "Henry," he is so safe!'

Lady Augusta Fane, *Chit Chat*, 1926

The hunting parson and the army officer provided copy for nineteenth-century hunting journalists. By Trollope's time the hunting parson was already criticized.

For myself I own that I like the hunting parson. I generally find him to be about the most pleasant man

[47]

in the field, with the most to say for himself, whether the talk be of hunting, politics, of literature, or of the country. He is never a hunting man unalloyed, unadulterated, and unmixed – a class of man which is perhaps of all classes the most tedious and heavy in hand.

But still I confess that the hunting parson seems to have made a mistake. He is kicking against the pricks, and running counter to that section of the world which should be his section. He is making himself to stink in the nostrils of his bishop, and is becoming a stumbling block, and a rock of offence to his brethren. It is bootless for him to argue, as I have here argued, that his amusement is in itself innocent, and that some openair recreation is necessary to him. Grant him that the bishops and old ladies are wrong and that he is right in principle, and still he will not be justified. Whatever may be our walk of life, no man can walk well who does not walk with the esteem of his fellows. Now those little walks by the covert sides – those pleasant little walks of which I am writing – are not, unfortunately, held to be estimable, or good for themselves, by English clergymen in general.

Hunting Sketches, 1865

Charles Kingsley enjoyed hunting; but he had his doubts.

I know He has made me a parish priest, and that it is the duty which is nearest, but did He too let me become a strong, daring, sporting wild man of the woods for nothing?

At his funeral the Bramshill Hunt servants stayed outside the churchyard to avoid the reporters.

Nevertheless, as late as 1913, Cosmo Gordon Lang, Archbishop of Canterbury, preached on the occasion of the dedication of a memorial window in honour of a clergyman killed in a hunting accident.

[48]

Some people might find it difficult to understand how there could be a close connection between hunting and the life of a Christian clergyman, [but hunting] was a form of sport which developed some of the finest qualities of human nature – courage, endurance, readiness to face risk, comradeship and honourable courtesies.

Devil-may-care army officers threatening to run over hounds remained the bane of every MFH near a garrison town. Jorrocks found them unstoppable.

'You 'air dresser on the chestnut horse,' he roars during a check, to a gentleman with a very big ginger moustache, 'pray 'old 'ard.'

'Hair dresser,' replies the gentleman, turning round in a fury, 'I'm an officer in the ninety-first regiment.'

'Then, you hossifer in the ninety-first regiment, wot looks like an 'air dresser, 'old 'ard.'

R. S. Surtees, *Handley Cross*, 1843

Hunting can damage growing crops and poach pasture. Its existence depends on the tolerance of farmers.

As we got nearer Downfield the country became more attractive-looking, and I estimated every fence we passed as if it had been put there for no other purpose than to be jumped by Harkaway. I had yet to become aware of the farmer's point of view. A large crowd of people riding over someone else's land and making holes in the hedges is likely to create all sorts of trouble for the Master of Hounds, but I had not thought of it in that way. The country was there to be ridden over. That was all. I knew that I ought to shut the gates behind me (and some of them were an awful nuisance to open, when Harkaway was excited), but it had not occurred to me that a hole in a fence through which fifty horses have blundered is much the same as an open gate, so far as the exodus of a farmer's cattle is concerned. However, this problem of trespassing by courtesy has existed as long as fox-hunting, and it is not likely to be solved until both the red-coated fraternity and the red-furred carnivorous mammal which they pursue have disappeared from England's green and pleasant land.

Siegfried Sassoon, *Memoirs of a Fox-Hunting Man*, 1928

It is not surprising that the tenant farmer who became an enthusiastic fox-hunter was much appreciated.

Lord Yarborough, the Brocklesbury Master, in a field that included sixty or seventy scarlet-coated tenant farmers, and being asked 'Where do you get your tenants?' and answering, 'I don't get 'em, I breed 'em'.

Jimmy Edwards, 'Rushing their Fences'
from *In Praise of Hunting*, 1960

Children are now conspicuous fox-hunters.

The hunt had begun to move off and the hounds were now flickering and undulating down the slope . . . They went through the gate and out on to the road. The rest of the hunt followed, roughly speaking in financial order, and a desultory cavalcade of children of varying ages, some of them mere infants, fought a sort of rear-guard action, dressed in jockey-caps and perched on saddles of every conceivable shape, some the basket Howdahs of donkeys on the beach, others of Spanish or Moorish patterns, recalling Mexico or the armies of the East. Among these walked or rode grooms, anxious men, trying to make the best of things. The horses clattered along the road and turned the corner so that after a few minutes all of them were out of sight behind the trees, except for one very pathetic child of inde-terminate sex, who, suddenly taken ill, had wisely decided to turn back with its keeper.

Anthony Powell, *From a View to a Death*, 1933

Although it was the social expansion of the hunting field beyond the narrow confines of the landed gentry that allowed it to survive, new entrants often had a hard time of it. A 'worthy citizen of Derby' begged a drink from Squire Pole of the Meynell.

'Try some,' the Squire said pleasantly – though re-senting the familiarity – at the same time offering his flask, at which the other took a long pull, thinking it was sure to be something good. But he made a wry face when he swallowed it, and a still sorrier one when the Squire said, laughing, 'And now I advise you to be off home as quick as you can. It's my gout mixture.'

J. Randall, *A History of the Meynell Hounds and Country*, 1901

Hunting Days

... a real good run seldom occurs ... for to get one requires so many circumstances combined – first, a good fox, then a good find and a good scent, then a good country, good luck etc. The chances against it are innumerable.

Tom Smith, *Extracts from the Diary of a Huntsman*, 1852

Fox-hunting was a rarity in the Middle Ages and the techniques employed were radically different from those employed from the 1800s to the present day. This description in Sir Gawain and the Green Knight *is one of the earliest descriptions of a fox-hunt in the fourteenth century.*

But the lord his custom keeps
And is early up and dressed.
After mass, he and his men made a small meal.
Merry was the morning; he demanded his horse.
The men were ready mounted before the main gate,
A host of knightly horsemen to follow after him.
Wonderfully fair was the forest-land, for the frost
    remained,
And the rising sun shone ruddily on the ragged clouds,
In its beauty brushing their blackness off the heavens.
The huntsmen unleashed the hounds by a holt-side,
And the rocks and surrounding bushes rang with
    their horn-calls.

Some found and followed the fox's tracks,
And wove various ways in their wily fashion.
A small hound cried the scent, the senior huntsman
    called
His fellow foxhounds to him and, feverishly sniffing,
The rout of dogs rushed forward on the right path.
The fox hurried fast, for they found him soon
And, seeing him distinctly, pursued him at speed,
Unmistakably giving tongue with tumultuous din.
Deviously in difficult country he doubled on his tracks,
Swerved and wheeled away, often waited listening,
Till at last by a little ditch he leaped a quickset hedge,
And stole out stealthily at the side of a valley,
Considering his stratagem had given the slip to the
    hounds.
But he stumbled on a tracking-dogs' tryst-place
    unawares,
And there in a cleft three hounds threatened him at
    once,
        All grey.
    He swiftly started back,
    And, full of deep dismay,
    He dashed on a different track;
    To the woods he went away.
Then came the lively delight of listening to hounds
When they had all met in a muster, mingling to–
    gether,
For, catching sight of him, they cried such curses on
    him
That the clustering cliffs seemed to be crashing down.
Here he was hallooed when the hunters met him,
There savagely snarled at by intercepting hounds;
Then he was called thief and threatened often;
With the tracking dogs on his tail, no tarrying was
    possible.

When out in the open he was often run at,
So he often swerved in again, that artful Reynard.
Yes, he led the lord and his liegemen a dance
In this manner among the mountains till mid-
    afternoon,
The prince was still on the plain, pleasuring in the
    chase,
Having finished off the fox he had followed so far.
As he leaped over a hedge looking out for the quarry,
Where he heard the hounds that were harrying the fox,
Reynard came running through a rough thicket
With the pack all pell-mell, panting at his heels.
The lord, aware of the wild beast, waited craftily,
Then drew his dazzling sword and drove at the fox.
The beast baulked at the blade to break sideways,
But a dog bounded at him before he could,
And right in front of the horse's feet they fell on him,
All worrying their wily prey with a wild uproar.
The lord quickly alighted and lifted him up,
Wrenched him beyond reach of the ravening fangs,
Held him high over his head and hallooed lustily,
While the angry hounds in hordes bayed at him.
Thither hurried the huntsmen with horns in plenty,
Sounding the rally splendidly till they saw their lord.
When the company of his court had come up to the kill,
All who bore bugles blew at once,
And the others without horns hallooed loudly.
The requiem that was raised for Reynard's soul
And the commotion made it the merriest meet ever,
       Men said.
    The hounds must have their fee:
    They pat them on the head,
    Then hold the fox; and he
    Is reft of his skin of red.
Then they set off for home, it being almost night,
Blowing their big horns bravely as they went.

Byron refers to Lord Chesterfield's aversion to fox-hunting as 'fit only for our English Bumpkin Gentlemen'.

A fox-hunt to a foreigner is strange;
  'Tis also subject to the double danger
Of tumbling first, and having in exchange
  Some pleasant jesting at the awkward stranger:
But Juan had been early taught to range
  The wilds, as doth an Arab turn'd avenger,
So that his horse, or charger, hunter, hack,
Knew that he had a rider on his back.

And now in this new field, with some applause,
  He clear'd hedge, ditch, and double post, and rail,
And never *craned*, and made but few '*faux pas*,'
  And only fretted when the scent 'gan fail.
He broke, 'tis true, some statutes of the laws
  Of hunting – for the sagest youth is frail;
Rode o'er the hounds, it may be, now and then,
And once o'er several country gentlemen.

But on the whole, to general admiration
  He acquitted both himself and horse: the squires
Marvell'd at merit of another nation;
  The boors cried 'Dang it! who'd have thought
        it?'—Sires,

The Nestors of the sporting generation,
  Swore praises, and recall'd their former fires;
The huntsman's self relented to a grin,
And rated him almost a whipper-in.
Such were his trophies – not of spear and shield,
  But leaps, and bursts, and sometimes foxes' brushes;
Yet I must own, – although in this I yield
  To patriot sympathy a Briton's blushes, –
He thought at heart like courtly Chesterfield,
  Who, after a long chase o'er hills, dales, bushes,
And what not, though he rode beyond all price,
Ask'd next day, 'If men ever hunted *twice*?'

He also had a quality uncommon
  To early risers after a long chase,
Who wake in winter ere the cock can summon
  December's drowsy day to his dull race, –
A quality agreeable to woman,
  When her soft, liquid words run on apace,
Who likes a listener, whether saint or sinner, –
He did not fall asleep just after dinner;

                    Don Juan, xxxii–xxxvi, 1822

Almost all Trollope's novels contain descriptions of fox-hunts. This describes the wise hound, Dido, finding a fox.

'By George, that's a fox! That's Dido! That's a find!'
And Spooner galloped away, as though Dido could do
nothing with the fox she had found unless he was there
to help her. Spooner was quite right, as he generally
was on such occasions. He knew the hounds even by
voice, and knew what hound he could believe. Most
hounds will lie occasionally, but Dido never lied. And
there were many besides Spooner who believed in
Dido. The whole pack rushed to her music, though the
body of them would have remained utterly unmoved at

the voice of any less reverenced and less trustworthy colleague. The whole wood was at once in commotion – men and women riding hither and thither, not in accordance with any judgment; but as they saw or thought they saw others riding who were supposed to have judgment. To get away well is so very much! And to get away well is often so very difficult! There are so many things of which the horseman is bound to think in that moment. Which way does the wind blow? And then, though a fox will not long run up wind, he will break covert up wind, as often as not. From which of the various rides can you find a fair exit into the open country, without a chance of breaking your neck before the run begins? When you hear some wild halloa, informing you that one fox has gone in the direction exactly opposite to that in which the hounds are hunting, are you sure that the noise is not made about a second fox? On all these matters you are bound to make up your mind without losing a moment; and if you make up your mind wrongly the five pounds you have invested in that day's amusement will have been spent for nothing.

Phineas Redux, 1874

In her lengthy memoirs of her husband Mrs Kingsley carefully left out his enthusiastic references to hunting.

... I had just done my work, and dinner was coming on the table yesterday – just four o'clock, – when the bow-wows appeared on the top of the Mount, trying my patch of gorse; so I jumped up, left the cook shrieking, and off. He wasn't there, but I knew where he was, for I keep a pretty good register of foxes (ain't they my parishioners, and parts of my flock?); and, as the poor fellows had had a blank, they were very thankful to find themselves in five minutes going like mad. We had an hour and a half of it – scent breast-high as the dew be-

gan to rise (bleak north-easter – always good weather),
and if we had not crossed a second fox, should have
killed him in the open; as it was we lost him after sun-
set, after the fiercest grind I have had this nine years,
and I went back to my dinner. The old horse behaved
beautifully; he is not fast, but in the enclosed wood-
lands he can live up to any one, and earned great
honour by leaping in and out of the Loddon; only four
more doing it, and one receiving a mucker. I feel three
years younger today. . . . The whip tells me there were
three in the river together, rolling over horse and man!
What a sight to have lost even by being a-head.

> Letter to T. Hughes.
> Charles Kingsley, *Letters and Memories*, 1877

*Cub-hunting in the autumn marks the beginning of the
fox-hunting year. It takes place in the early morning.*

The happiest man in England rose an hour before the
    dawn;
The stars were in the purple and the dew was on the
    lawn;
He sang from bed to bathroom – he could only sing
    'John Peel';
He donned his boots and breeches and he buckled on
    his steel.

He chose his brightest waistcoat and his stock with
    care he tied,
Though scarce a soul would see him in his early
    morning ride.
He hurried to the stable through the dim light of the
    stars,
And there his good horse waited, clicking rings and
    bridle-bars.

The happiest man in England took a grey lock in his
hand
And settled in his saddle like a seagull on the sand.
Then from the shadowy kennel all the eager pack
outpoured,
And the happiest man in England saw them scatter
on the sward.

The happiest man in England turned down the stony
lane,
The heart of him was singing as he heard the hoofs
again;
And where the blind ditch narrows and the deep-set
gorse begins
He waved his pack to covert, and he cheered them
through the whins.

He heard old Gladsome whimper, then Merryman
give tongue;
He saw the green gorse shaking as the whole pack
checked and swung;
Then through the ditch came creeping a shy cub
lithe and lean,
And nothing but a cocked grey ear betrayed that he
was seen.

But once beyond the brambles and across the heath
and clear
With half a league of open ground and not a whin-
bush near,
The happiest man in England blew the freedom of
the pass,
And two-and-twenty couple backed his music on the
grass.

*　　*　　*

He holds no brief for slaughter, but the cubs must
take their chance
The weak must first go under that the strong may
lead the dance;
And when the grey strides out and shakes the foam-
flecks from his rings
The happiest man in England would not change his
place with kings.

W. H. Ogilvie, *The Happiest Man in England*, 1925

*Edith Somerville and Martin Ross hunted in Ireland.
They were less starry-eyed.*

I had gone through the dreary routine of the cub-
hunter. The alarm clock had shrilled its exulting and
age-long summons in the pitchy dark. I had burnt my
fingers with the spirit-lamp, and my mouth with hot
cocoa; I had accomplished my bathless toilet, I had
groped my way through the puddles in the stable yard,
and got on to my horse by the light of a lantern, and at
5.30 a.m. I was over the worst, and had met Flurry and
the hounds . . . at the appointed cross-roads.

It was still an hour before sunrise, but a pallor was
in the sky, and the hounds, that had at first been like a
gliding shoal of fish round the horses' feet, began to
take on their own shapes and colours.

E. Œ. Somerville and Martin Ross,
Further Experiences of an Irish R.M., 1917

In a letter of 1887 to Martin Ross, Edith Somerville describes the excitements of being alone with hounds. A is her brother, Aylmer.

So A and I made a hurried guess by the look of things at the way he was running, and set off as hard as we could lick round the bog, on a bog road. One local genius was with us but after we got round the bog he turned off to the east and we saw him no more. We had a moment of agony as to whether we would follow him but decided to go our own way. And it was well for us.

We went on for about 5 minutes, best pace, when a country boy began to roar at us, something about going to the west (we were riding NW) over the bog. We turned sharp off, Sorcerer nearly pulling my arms out, he was so excited, when we heard something. My dear, about 100 yards back to the south we saw the *whole pack* come streaming down the hill, without a man within a mile of them. It was the fox only who had gone across to the west. When they got to the road we had just left, they checked. Then was our time. We rode down like mad, whipped them onto the line the fox had gone, and off they went again, full cry, with A and I *alone* after them. It was almost too supreme a moment. I could not have spoken, except in a sort of mad howl to the hounds, to save my life and I could hardly see. However they ran over a country where you had to see. We were just going about as hard as the horses could leg it, but the hounds were racing with their heads up and the scent red hot. It was all we could do to keep them in sight over that breakneck place, but we did somehow and in about 20 minutes they checked round a huge cairn of stones. A nipped off and climbed round to get the fox out, when suddenly before you could say knife out jumped the fox into the very jaws of the whole

[61]

pack. He had been in a tunnel and A had started him out. The hounds were so taken by surprise that they hadn't time to nail him and out, *literally*, between their legs he slipped and away with him with the hounds, A and me, all blue with passion, after him. But he knew what he was up to. In about 1 or 2 hundred yards there was a big rock and he just wriggled into it as the leading hound made a snap at his brush. I couldn't have believed anything could have got away as he did. I am generally glad when a game fox gets off, but I must admit that A and I could have cried. We thought we were sure of the brush. There we stood and stared at each other.

Maurice Collis, *Somerville and Ross*, 1968

A kill.

'WHO-HOOP!' shrieked Romford, in a voice that made the hills ring and reverberate. '*Who-hoop!*' repeated he, throwing himself from his horse, and diving into the midst of the pack, to extricate the fox from their fangs. Up he held him triumphantly, with the baying pack jumping and frolicking around. 'Take my horse away now,' cried Facey to Swig, and the coast being then clear, Facey advanced a few steps to where a soft mossy bank seemed to invite the performance of the last obsequies of the chase. There on the bright green cushion he cast the nut-brown fox.

Meanwhile, the field having availed themselves of the facilities of Beltingford Bridge, were now making the air and the hard road ring with their voices and the noise of their horses' hoofs, all in a deuce of a stew lest they should lose the hounds, or not be up at the kill. They had not yet arrived at the elegant point of indifference that makes men turn their horses' heads homewards as soon as they hear 'who-hoop!' and most satisfactory (though of course none of them admitted it) Romford's death-note sounded on their ears.

They had all about had enough. The gallant Captain Spurrier had lost a shoe, Mr Blanton had lost two, while Mr James Allnut and his son had lost five between them.

Mr Romford took no advantage of their circumlocution, but keeping the fox on the green bank, maintained the ardour of the pack by repeated hoops and halloos. So there was a very lively circle when the last of the field came up. Facey and the fox in the centre, the baying hounds all around, Chowey and Swig outside, contributing their occasional quota of noise to the scene.

'Well (puff) done!' exclaimed Mr Bullpig, mopping himself.

'Capital (gasp) run!' shouted Allnut, who had only seen half of it.

'Never saw better (puff) hounds in my life!' asserted Mr Large, who had never seen any but the Surrey.

Then all having come up, Chowey, at a signal from Facey, proceeded to divest the fox of his brush and his pads, prior to presenting the remainder to the hounds. Up then went the carcase, which was caught by a myriad of mouths as it fell. Tear him and eat him, was then the cry. And tear him and eat him they did. The master of the circle, Facey Romford, then quitted the ring, now somewhat difficult to maintain in consequence of the struggling efforts of the fox-devouring hounds, and having decorated Master Allnut's pony with the brush, and given the pads to those who would have them, proceeded to the outer ring, to hear how things were going on there.

There was a great discussion about the time and distance.

Mr Pyefinch said it was nine miles as the crow flies. Doctor Snuff, who had joined promiscuously on a

cob, thought it was hardly that, but it was a good eight.

Mr Kickton thought it was more than eight. It was seven to Stewley Hill, and the rocks were two good miles beyond it.

Then they appealed to Mr Romford.

'How far should you say it was, Mr Romford?' demanded Mr Joseph Large, who thought he had come twenty at least.

'Faith, I've no notion!' replied Facey, adding, 'He was a right good fox, any how.'

'Capital!' ejaculated Mr Large, adding, 'It was almost a pity to kill him.'

'Not a bit,' retorted Facey, 'always kill 'em when you can. The more you kill, the more you'll have to kill.'

The teapot-handle-maker didn't understand that doctrine, but took it for granted. He inwardly hoped there were not many such foxes in the country.

Then Facey, pretending that the run was nothing out of the way, remounted his horse, demanding where they should go next; whereupon they all cried 'Content!' recommending him to go home and change, for he must be very wet, and began asking their own individual ways, for some people will live in a country all their lives, and yet never know where they are after hunting.

R. S. Surtees, *Mr Facey Romford's Hounds*, 1865

John Masefield understood fox-hunting as a non-hunting countryman. He describes a hunt through a foot-follower's eyes.

They saw the Yell Brook like a gem
Blue in the grass a short mile on
They heard faint cries, but hounds were gone
A good eight fields and out of sight
Except a rippled glimmer white
Going away with dying cheering
And scarlet flappings disappearing,
And scattering horses going, going,
Going like mad, White Rabbit snowing
Far on ahead, a loose horse taking,
Fence after fence with stirrups shaking,
And scarlet specks and dark specks dwindling.

Nearer, were twigs knocked into kindling,
A much bashed fence still dropping stick,
Flung clods, still quivering from the kick,
Cut hoof-marks pale in cheesy clay,
The horse-smell blowing clean away.
Birds flitting back into the cover.
One last faint cry, then all was over.
The hunt had been, and found, and gone.

Reynard the Fox, 1919

A run from the fox's point of view.

Then again the kettle drum horse hooves beat,
And the green blades bent to the fox's feet
And the cry rose keen not far behind
Of the 'Blood, blood, blood' in the fox-hounds' mind.

The fox was strong, he was full of running,
He could run for an hour and then be cunning,
But the cry behind him made him chill,
They were nearer now and they meant to kill.
They meant to run him until his blood
Clogged on his heart as his brush with mud,
Till his back bent up and his tongue hung flagging,
And his belly and brush were filthed from dragging.
Till he crouched stone still, dead-beat and dirty,
With nothing but teeth against the thirty.

And all the way to that blinding end
He would meet with men and have none his friend.
Men to holloa and men to run him,
With stones to stagger and yells to stun him,
Men to head him, with whips to beat him,
Teeth to mangle and mouths to eat him.
And all the way, that wild high crying,
To cold his blood with the thought of dying,
The horn and the cheer, and the drum-like thunder,
Of the horse hooves stamping the meadows under.
He upped his brush and went with a will
For the Sarsen Stones on Wan Dyke Hill.

John Masefield, Reynard the Fox, 1919

Going Home.

. . . Those were the days when everyone rode home,
there was no riding then to the nearest telephone and
waiting for the car to pick you up. Riding home after a

hard day has been sufficiently described, every fox-
hunter brings it in to one of his books. It is like coming
after football to a hot bath, it has been hard exercise in
the open and you feel what you so often hear described
'that delicious feeling of tiredness'. Feelings of that
kind depend on peace of mind, they are luxuries for
those used to luxury. No more than hard exercise will
give a sense of work well done. As such it is enough to
entrance little boys, to make them feel important.

On hunting days we had eggs for tea, just as our
parents did, and this was the first sign of growing up.

Henry Green, *Pack My Bag*, 1940

*After dinner post-mortems of the day's run, inflicted on
the unwary, early created the hunting bore.*

For happy he who tops the wheeling chase;
Has every maze evolved, and every guile
Disclosed; who knows the merits of the pack;
Who saw the villain seized, and dying hard
Without complaint, though by an hundred mouths
Relentless torn: O glorious he beyond
His daring peers, when the retreating horn
Calls them to ghostly halls of grey renown,
With woodland honours graced – the fox's fur
Depending decent from the roof, and spread
Round the drear walls, with antic figures fierce,
The stag's large front: he then is loudest heard
When the night staggers with severer toils,
With feats Thessalian Centaurs never knew,
And their repeated wonders shake the dome.

James Thomson, *The Seasons*, 1730

Dining, and passing the whole evening, with a party of
fox-hunters, after they have had what they call 'glorious
sport'; and, while you execrate the very name of a
hound, being gorged with the *crambe recocta* of one

fox-chase after another, till, like Miss Larolles, you 'wish the country was under ground.'

Anon., *The Miseries of Human Life* (4th edition, 1806),
'The sixty-fifth misery'

Fox-hunters are catastrophists, always in fear that their sport is on the point of destruction by some advance of modern civilization: the spread of towns; railways; cars.

Bricks and mortar have played havoc with much good fox-hunting country, even since the Great War, and doubtless the Old Berkeley Foxhounds would gladly forget that their country, technically, includes parts not only of the suburbs of London but also of London itself. How Tom Oldaker, huntsman to Lord Berkeley at the end of the eighteenth century, found a fox at Wormwood Scrubs (even then giving shelter to marauders) and lost him close to Kensington Gardens has become almost a boring story.

But another incident of the same period is worth recalling. 'No fox was found in Kensington Gardens after 1798,' says 'The Druid,' 'when the gardeners combined against two litters in the sewer "for carrying off water into the fosse under the upper bastion", and shot one of their own body in their undisciplined ardour.' It is not often that we hear now of such a heavy bag – two litters of cubs and a gardener – after any corresponding *battue*.

Foxhunting from the Times, 1933

Kipling makes the fox speak.

> When Pigg and Jorrocks held the stage,
>   And Steam had linked the Shires,
> I broke the staid Victorian age
>   To posts, and rails and wires.

[68]

Then fifty mile was none too far
    To go by train to cover,
Till some dam' sutler pupped a Car,
    And decent sport was over!

When men grew shy of hunting stag
    For fear the Law might try 'em,
The car put up an average bag
    Of twenty dead per diem.
Then every road was made a rink
    For Coroners to sit on;
And so began, in skid and stink,
    The real blood-sports of Britain!

The Fox Meditates

Lady Augusta Fane on cars:

In spite of their obvious utility, motor cars have spoilt hunting. They enable a crowd of strangers to hunt where they do not live, and where they consequently spend no money and do no good to the farmers. Tarmac roads are most dangerous for horses, as they cannot get a foothold on a wet day, and there have been many serious accidents from horses slipping and falling on their riders. Much good fellowship has been lost now hacking to covert has ended. The country roads are no longer quiet and peaceful, and it is hard to find any place that is free of noise and the smell of petrol. I often long for the scent of fresh hay in a stable and the soft whinnying of one's favourite hunter for the expected carrot; instead I am led into a stuffy garage with the chauffeur running the engines! This is a mechanical age, the youngest children know the name of every car and talk learnedly of the difference between a Rolls and Buick, and the moment anybody arrives on a visit he or she recounts excitedly how many hundred miles they have done in a couple of hours! As if it could possibly matter or be of the slightest interest.

Chit Chat, 1926

Modern Masters have realized the financial support of car followers outweighs any interference with sport. Captain Wallace was Master of the Heythrop, now of the Exmoor Foxhounds.

Ronnie Wallace is unfailingly courteous to people on foot and in cars. Many Masters treat them with fair contempt, but they are a source of income which he has organised into a very profitable supporters club. Followers come . . . jamming the lanes, spoiling the scent with their exhausts, perhaps, but always welcome. It is with hunt members that Wallace can be crushing. 'He is terrifying' says one. 'It's not what he says, which isn't much. It's the way it's spat out, and with a glare that seems to stick with you all day. Rich, powerful people with no need to take any stick, can be very frightened of Wallace.'

Brian Moynahan, *Leader of the Pack*

Joys

'. . . dear, delightful 'unting the werry mention of whose name kivers me with the creeps, and thrills me all over with joy'.

Jorrocks in R. S. Surtees, *Handley Cross*, 1843

The great fox-hunting classic is Beckford's Thoughts upon Hunting, *written in 1781 when fox-hunting was replacing hare-hunting as the normal occupation of the country gentleman.*

Fox-hunting, an acquaintance of mine says, is only to be followed because you can ride hard, and do less harm in that than in any other kind of hunting. There may be some truth in the observation; but, to such as love the riding part only of hunting, would not a trail-scent be more suitable? Gentlemen who hunt for the sake of a ride, who are indifferent about the hounds, and know little of the business, if they do no harm, fulfil as much as we have reason to expect from them; whilst those of a contrary disposition do good, and have much greater pleasure. Such as are acquainted with the hounds, and can at times assist them, find the sport more interesting, and frequently have the satisfaction to think, that they themselves contribute to the success of the day. This is a pleasure that you often enjoy; a pleasure without any regret attending it. . . . I know not what effect it may have on you; but I know that my spirits are always good after good sport in hunting; nor is the rest of the day ever disagreeable to me. What are other sports, compared with this, which is full of enthusiasm! – Fishing is, in my opinion, a dull diversion; shooting, though it admit of a companion, will not allow of many: – both, therefore, may be considered as selfish and solitary amusements, compared with hunting; to which as many as please are welcome: – the one might teach patience to a philosopher; and the other, though it occasion great fatigue to the body, seldom affords much occupation to the mind; whereas *fox-hunting is a kind of warfare*; its uncertainties, its fatigues, its difficulties, and its dangers, rendering it interesting above all other diversions.

Beckford was a purist. The excitement of the chase should not obscure its main object : killing foxes.

Sport is but a secondary consideration with a true fox-hunter. The first is *the killing of the fox*: hence arises the eagerness of pursuit – chief pleasure of the chase. I confess, I esteem blood so necessary to a pack of foxhounds, that, with regard to myself, I always return home better pleased with but an indifferent chase, with death at the end of it, than with the best chase possible, if it end with the loss of the fox. Good chases, generally speaking, are long chases; and, if not attended with success, never fail to do more harm to hounds than good. Our pleasures, I believe, for the most part, are greater during the expectation than the enjoyment. In this case, reality itself warrants the idea, and your present success is almost a sure fore-runner of future sport.

P. Beckford, *Thoughts upon Hunting*, 1781

To Nimrod (1779–1843) the sporting journalist, the excitements of hunting in a fast grass country made the Shires 'the eye of hunting England'. Here is a modern description of Shire hunting.

Those who have done all their riding on lazy school hacks have no hint of the power of a corned up Leicestershire hunter. It is the difference between riding a bicycle and driving a Jaguar.

Lord Stalbridge: 'The hardest and best-mounted riders in the world behind, and all grass and big fences in front.'

I myself have hunted occasionally as the rankest of novices, and never from Saigon to the Cresta Run have I known such terror. There is a moment of ignition when hounds start to run, and the mad scramble across country begins. Sense, manners and (in my case) all control are lost. Fences and fields rush up in busy succession. The exhilaration of surviving seems enough.

Max Hastings, *The Observer*, 23 November 1980

We offer no apologies for the inclusion of that lengthy classic W. Bromley Davenport's The Dream of the Old Meltonian *(1864). Melton Mowbray was the winter headquarters of the smart hunting fraternity.*

I am old, I am old, and my eyes are grown weaker,
My beard is as white as the foam on the sea,
Yet pass me the bottle and fill me a beaker,
A bright brimming toast in a bumper for me!
Back, back, through long vistas of years I am wafted,
But the glow at my heart's undiminished in force;
Deep, deep in that heart has fond memory engrafted
Those quick thirty minutes from Ranksboro' Gorse.

What is time? The effluxion of life zoophitic
In dreary pursuit of position or gain.
What is life? The absorption of vapours mephitic,
And the burning of sunlight on senses and brain!
Such a life have I lived – though so speedily over,
Condensing the joys of a century's course,
From the find till we beat him near Woodwellhead
    Cover,
In thirty bright minutes from Ranksboro' Gorse.

Last night in St Stephen's so wearily sitting
(The member for Boreham sustained the debate,)
Some pitying spirit that round me was flitting
Vouchsafed a sweet vision my pains to abate.
The Mace, and the Speaker, the House disappearing,
The leather-clad bench is a thoroughbred horse;
'Tis the whimpering cry of the foxhound I'm hearing,
And my 'seat' is a pigskin at Ranksboro' Gorse.

He's away! I can hear the identical holloa!
I can feel my young thoroughbred strain down the
    ride,
I can hear the dull thunder of hundreds that follow,
I can see my old comrades in life by my side.
Do I dream? All around me I see the dead riding,
And voices long silent re-echo with glee;
I can hear the far wail of the Master's vain chiding,
As vain as the Norseman's reproof to the sea.

Vain, indeed! for the bitches are racing before us –
Not a nose to the earth, not a stern in the air;
And we know by the notes of that modified chorus
How straight we must ride if we wish to be there!
With a crash o'er the turnpike, and onward I'm
    sailing,
Released from the throes of the blundering mass,
Which dispersed right and left as I topped the high
    railing,
And shaped my own course o'er the billowy grass.

Select is the circle in which I am moving,
Yet open and free the admission to all;
Still, still more select is that company proving,
Weeded out by the funker, and thinned by the fall:
Yet here all are equal – no class legislation,
No privilege hinders, no family pride:
In the 'image of war' show the pluck of the nation;
Ride, ancient patrician! democracy, ride!

Oh! gently, my young one; the fence we are nearing
Is leaning towards us – 'tis hairy and black,
The binders are strong, and necessitate clearing,
Or the wide ditch beyond will find room for your
    back.
Well saved! we are over! now far down the pastures
Of Ashwell the willows betoken the line,
Of the dull-flowing stream of historic disasters
We must face, my bold young one, the dread
    Whissendine.

No shallow-dug pan with a hurdle to screen it,
That cocktail imposture, the steeplechase brook:
But the steep broken banks tells us plain, if we mean
    it,
The less we shall like it the longer we look.

[75]

Then steady, my young one, my place I've selected,
Above the dwarf willow, 'tis sound I'll be bail,
With your muscular quarters beneath you collected
Prepare for a rush like the 'limited mail.'

Oh! now let me know the full worth of your breeding;
Brave son of Belzoni, be true to your sires,
Sustain old traditions – remember you're leading
The cream of the cream in the shire of the shires!

Though a rough-riding world may bespatter your
    breeches,
Though sorrow may cross you or slander revile,
Though you plunge overhead in misfortune's blind
    ditches,
Shun the gap of deception, the handgate of guile:
Oh, avoid them! for there see the crowd is contending,
Ignoble the object – ill-mannered the throng;
Shun the miry lane, falsehood, with turns never ending,
Ride straight for truth's timber, no matter how strong.

I'll pound you safe over! sit steady and quiet,
Along the sound headland of honesty steer;
Beware of false holloas and juvenile riot:
Though the oxer of duty be wide, never fear!

And when the run's over of earthly existence,
And you get safe to ground, you will feel no remorse,
If you ride it – no matter what line or what distance –
As straight as your fathers from Ranksboro' Gorse.

With a quick, shortened stride as the distance you
     measure
With a crack of the nostril and cock of the ear,
And a rocketing bound, and we're over, my treasure,
Twice nine feet of water, and landed all clear.

What! four of us only? Are these the survivors
Of all that rode gaily from Ranksboro' ridge?
I hear the faint splash of a few hardy divers,
The rest are in hopeless research of a bridge;
Vae Victis! the way of the world and the winners!
Do we ne'er ride away from a friend in distress?
Alas! we are anti-Samaritan sinners,
And streaming past Stapleford, onward we press.

Ah! don't they mean mischief, the merciless ladies?
What fox can escape such implacable foes?
Of the sex cruel slaughter for ever the trade is,
Whether human or animal – YONDER HE GOES!
Never more for the woodland! his purpose has failed
     him,
Though to gain the old shelter he gallantly tries;
In vain the last double, for Jezebel's nailed him!
WHO-WHOOP! in the open the veteran dies!

Yes, four of us only! But is it a vision?
Dear lost ones, how come ye with mortals to mix?
Methought that ye hunted the pastures Elysian,
And between us there rolled the unjumpable Styx!

Stay, stay but a moment! the grass fields are fading,
And heavy obscurity palsies my brain:
Through what country, what ploughs and what
    sloughs am I wading?
Alas! 'tis the member for Boreham again!

Oh! glory of youth! consolation of age!
Sublimest of ecstasies under the sun;
Though the veteran may linger too long on the stage,
Yet he'll drink a last toast to a fox-hunting run.
And oh! young descendants of ancient top-sawyers!
By your lives to the world their example enforce;
Whether landlords, or parsons, or statesmen, or
    lawyers,
Ride straight as they rode it from Ranksboro' Gorse.

*The novelist Anthony Trollope (1815–82) discovered the
joys of fox-hunting when he was sent to Ireland as a Post
Office official in 1841.*

I found that the surveyor to whom I had been sent kept
a pack of hounds, and therefore I bought a hunter. I do
not think he liked it, but he could not well complain.
He never rode to hounds himself, but I did; and then
and thus began one of the great joys of my life. I have
ever since been constant to the sport, having learned to
love it with an affection which I cannot myself fathom
or understand. Surely no man has laboured at it as I
have done, or hunted under such drawbacks as to
distances, money, and natural disadvantages. I am very
heavy, very blind, have been – in reference to hunting
– a poor man, and am now an old man. I have often
had to travel all night outside a mail-coach, in order
that I might hunt the next day. Nor have I ever been
in truth a good horseman. And I have passed the greater
part of my hunting life under the discipline of the Civil

Service. But it has been for more than thirty years a
duty to me to ride to hounds; and I have performed that
duty with a persistent energy. Nothing has ever been
allowed to stand in the way of hunting, – neither the
writing of books, nor the work of the Post Office, nor
other pleasures. As regarded the Post Office, it soon
seemed to be understood that I was to hunt; and when
my services were re-transferred to England, no word of
difficulty ever reached me on the subject. I have
written on very many subjects, and on most of them
with pleasure; but on no subject with such delight as
that of hunting. I have dragged it into many novels, –
into too many no doubt, – but I have always felt myself deprived of a legitimate joy when the nature of the
tale has not allowed me a hunting chapter.

Autobiography, 1883

*Charles Darwin's interest in natural history followed from
his love of sport. On receiving confirmation of the voyage
of the* Beagle *he wrote to a friend :*

What changes I have had. Till one today I was building
castles in the air about hunting foxes in Shropshire,
now llamas in South America.

Life and Letters of Charles Darwin,
ed. Norah Bellow, 1958

Reflecting on his hunting days he wrote :

Although as we shall presently see there were some re-
deeming features in my life at Cambridge, my time was
sadly wasted there and worse than wasted. From my
passion for shooting and for hunting and when this
failed, for riding across the country, I got into a sporting set, including some dissipated low-minded young
men. We used to dine together in the evening, though
these dinners often included men of a higher stamp,
and we sometimes drank too much, with jolly singing

[79]

and playing at cards afterwards. I know that I ought to feel ashamed of days and evenings thus spent, but as some of my friends were very pleasant and we were all in the highest spirits I cannot help looking back to these times with much pleasure.

The Autobiography of Charles Darwin,
ed. Francis Darwin, 1887

W. S. Blunt, country squire, poet, and champion of the Third World, describes the pleasures of hare hunting, on his Sussex estate. Many modern fox-hounds descend from packs of harriers.

I like the calm of the early fields,
The ducks asleep by the lake,
The quiet hour which Nature yields,
Before mankind is awake.

I like the pheasants and feeding things
Of the unsuspicious morn;
I like the flap of the wood-pigeon's wings
As she rises from the corn.

I like the blackbird's shriek, and his rush
From the turnips as I pass by,
And the partridge hiding her head in a bush,
For her young ones cannot fly.

I like these things, and I like to ride
When all the world is in bed,
To the top of the hill where the sky grows wide,
And where the sun grows red.

W. S. Blunt, *The Old Squire*, 1914

The joys of hunting were incomprehensible to Trollope's American Senator, Mr Gotobed.

'Now they are hunting,' said Mr Morton to the Senator.

'They all seemed to be very angry with each other at that narrow gate.'

'They were in a hurry, I suppose.'

'Two of them jumped over the hedge. Why didn't they all jump? How long will it be now before they catch him?'

'Very probably they may not catch him at all.'

'Not catch him after all that! Then the man was certainly right to poison that other fox in the wood. How long will they go on?'

'Half an hour perhaps.'

'And you call that hunting! Is it worth the while of all those men to expend all that energy for such a result? Upon the whole, Mr Morton, I should say that it is one of the most incomprehensible things that I have ever seen in the course of a rather long and varied life. Shooting I can understand, for you have your birds. Fishing I can understand, as you have your fish. Here you get a fox to begin with, and are all broken-hearted. Then you come across another, after riding about all day, and the chances are you can't catch him!'

'I suppose,' said Mr Morton angrily, 'the habits of one country are incomprehensible to the people of another. When I see Americans loafing about in the bar-room of an hotel, I am lost in amazement.'

'There is not a man you see who couldn't give a reason for his being there. He has an object in view, – though perhaps it may be no better than to rob his neighbour. But here there seems to be no possible motive.'

But just at that moment, while the hounds and the master, and Lord Rufford and his friends, were turning back in their own direction, John Morton came up with his carriage and the Senator. 'Is it all over?' asked the Senator.

'All over for to-day,' said Lord Rufford.

'Did you catch the animal?'

'No, Mr Gotobed; we couldn't catch him. To tell the truth we didn't try; but we had a nice little skurry for four or five miles.'

'Some of you look very wet.' Captain Glomax and Ned Botsey were standing near the carriage; but the Captain as soon as he heard this, broke into a trot and followed the hounds.

'Some of us are very wet,' said Ned. 'That's part of the fun.'

'Oh; – that's part of the fun. You found one fox dead and you didn't kill another because you didn't try. Well; Mr Morton, I don't think I shall take to fox hunting even though they should introduce it in Mickewa. What's become of the rest of the men?'

'Most of them are in the brook,' said Net Botsey ...

The American Senator, 1877

The obsessional fox-hunter's conception of happiness remains remote from that of ordinary mortals.

A story is told of a veteran sportsman who was asked upon one occasion as to what he thought were the three most enjoyable things in the world. As to what was the best, he had no doubt, it was a good day with hounds. He hesitated a little before replying to the query as what was the next best thing, but it was only for a short time, and then he replied, 'A bad day with hounds.' What was the third best thing was a bit of a poser after that, but after a long and careful consideration he shouted out to his tormentor in answer to the question '——it, sir, a blank day with hounds.'

W. Scarth Dixon, *The Sport of Kings*, 1900

Catastrophes

'A toss is a hawful thing.'

Jorrocks in R. S. Surtees, *Handley Cross*, 1843

No game was ever worth a rap
For a rational man to play,
In which no accident, no mishap,
Could possibly find its way.

Adam Lindsay Gordon, *Ye Wearie Wayfarer*, 1894

... and sport's like life and life's like sport,
It ain't all skittles and beer.

Ibid.

I love hunting, but I fear leaping. A King and the
father of a family should not ride bold.

George III

*Fox-hunting is often dull, sometimes comic, and sometimes
tragic. Two early disasters in the history of one of the
first regular fox-hunts, the Charlton Hunt formed by
Mr Roper, a supporter of the Duke of Monmouth.*

A Fox just found; gett on he cried! and then
That Instant fell, and Life that instant fled
And thus Ropero died at Eighty-four
A quick and sudden death, and in the field
Could Julius Caesar ere have wisht for more?

*   *   *

That vilest slave, the Huntsman, Ware his name
Alone and drunk, went out and let the pack
Kill fourteen farmer's sheep, all in one day.

The Earl of March, *Records of the Charlton Hunt*, 1910

*Mr John Corbet's hounds ended up in Lady Hertford's
ornamental dairy.*

The pack, heedless of the damsel's scream
First ate the fox – then drank the cream.

'Venator', *The Warwickshire Hunt from
1795 to 1836*

From Nimrod's Riding to Hounds:

When I was about eighteen years of age, I had a narrow
escape from being drowned with Mr Leech's hounds.
The hounds crossed the river Dee – naturally a very
rapid river, but then increased by the rains. Sir Watkin
Wynn, who (as well as his two brothers) is like a duck
in the water, went first, and was followed by about six
out of the field. 'Half venturing, half shrinking', I went
a little way into the stream, and came back again.
Seeing the hounds hitting off their fox on the other
side, I made a second attempt; and being mounted on
a mare of Sir Watkin's, called *Thetis*, and trusting to
her *genii* to preserve me, I made a second attempt, and
was carried down the stream amongst some huge
stones. Not being able to swim, I gave myself up for
lost; but the resolution of the mare, and my holding on
by the mane, enabled her to regain the opposite bank,
and I have never tried such an aquatic excursion since.
A man may attempt the Hellespont for a woman; but,
on cooler reflection, he is scarcely justified in running
such risks of his life for a fox.

The Newby Ferry Disaster.

On 4 February 1869, the York and Ainsty hounds met at Stainley House. They soon chopped one fox, and found another at Greenwood's Whin (or one account says Monckton Whin). After running for about an hour the fox crossed the River Ure opposite Newby Hall. The stream was in flood and was sixty yards wide, but the hounds crossed in safety, after being all washed down over the weir two hundred yards below. The ford below the weir was impassable owing to the flood, so Sir Charles Slingsby, the Master, hailed the ferry boat, which was worked on a chain four hundred yards above the weir. Two Newby Hall gardeners, father and son, called Warriner, pulled the boat across.

One spectator says that the boat should not have held more than three horses, but in the excitement of the moment it was at once overloaded, and when it was pushed off again it contained thirteen men and eleven horses. . . .

Some say that the trouble was begun by Sir Charles's horse, an old favourite called Saltfish, kicking Sir George Wombwell's horse. Anyhow, there was some disturbance, and Saltfish jumped overboard, pulling his master with him. Sir Charles struck out for the shore, and Saltfish followed him 'like a dog.' He had almost reached the bank when he got into difficulties, just failed to grasp Saltfish by the mane, and disappeared. Meanwhile the ferry boat had rocked (some say that it began to fill with water even before it was loaded), and since by some mischance the chain was on the downstream side the current caught the upstream edge and overturned it.

Seven minutes more saw the end of the tragedy. Captain Key had foreseen the danger of capsizing and, jumping out, reached the bank along the chain. Of the others, trapped underneath among the horses, the first to reappear was Mr Clare Vyner, who with great presence of mind scrambled on to the upturned boat and quickly pulled out Sir George Wombwell (who could not swim), Captain C. Molyneux, Major Mussenden (who had been kicked on the head by one of the horses), and Mr White (elsewhere reported to have reached the bank by the chain). Captain H. Molyneux, a sailor, swam ashore.

Mr Robinson, one of the best horsemen in England of that day, had never dismounted, and reappeared downstream still in the saddle, but his horse seemed to be unable to swim and they both sank. Mr Lloyd's case was the worst. He swam well, and with the aid of Captain Robert Vyner and Mr William Ingilby, who bravely came to his rescue, had almost reached the bank. But he was a very heavy man (also a fine horseman for his weight), and when he found that he was exhausted and that they could not tow him he gallantly let go and disappeared. Charles Orvis was carried downstream insensible, and the two gardeners, who are presumed to have been kicked by the horses, were never seen again alive.

Foxhunting from the Times, 1933

Trollope on the miseries of jumping into a field and being unable to jump out.

To get into a field, and then to have no way of getting out, is very uncomfortable. As long as you are on the road you have a way open before you to every spot on the world's surface – open, or capable of being opened; or even if incapable of being opened, not positively detrimental to you as long as you are on the right side. But that feeling of a prison under the open air is very terrible, and is rendered almost agonizing by the prisoner's consciousness that his position is the result of his own imprudent temerity – of an audacity which falls short of any efficacious purpose. When hounds are running, the hunting man should always, at any rate, be able to ride on – to ride in some direction, even though it be in the wrong direction. He can then flatter himself that he is riding wide and making a line for himself. But to be entrapped into a field without any power of getting out of it; to see the red backs of the forward men becoming smaller and smaller in the distance, till the last speck disappears over some hedge; to see the fence before you and know that it is too much for you; to ride round and round in an agony of despair which is by no means mute, and at last to give sixpence to some boy to conduct you back into the road; that is wretched – that is real unhappiness. I am, therefore, very persistent in my advice to the man who purposes to hunt without jumping. Let him not jump at all. To jump, but only jump a little, is fatal.

Hunting Sketches, 1865

The courageous Londoner who found time to warn his companions before he rode into a quarry.

'WARE HOLES

A sportin' death! My word it was!
An' taken in a sportin' way.
Mind you, I wasn't there to see;
I only tell you what they say.

'E was a stranger to the 'unt,
There weren't a person as 'e knew there;
But 'e could ride, that London gent –
'E sat 'is mare at if 'e grew there.

They seed the 'ounds upon the scent,
But found a fence across their track,
An' 'ad to fly it, else it meant
A turnin' an' a 'arking back.

'E was the foremost at the fence,
And as 'is mare just cleared the rail
'E turned to them that rode be'ind,
For three was at 'is very tail.

' 'Ware 'oles!' says 'e, an' with the word
Still sittin' easy on 'is mare,
Down, down 'e went, an' down an' down,
Into the quarry yawnin' there.

Some say it was two 'undred foot,
The bottom lay as black as ink.
I guess they 'ad some ugly dreams
Who reined their 'orses on the brink.

'E'd only time for that one cry;
' 'Ware 'oles!' says 'e, an' saves all three.
There may be better deaths to die,
But that one's good enough for me.

For, mind you, 'twas a sportin' end,
Upon a right good sportin' day;
They think a deal of 'im down 'ere,
That gent that came from London way.

Sir Arthur Conan Doyle, 1898

The dangers to a jumping horse of wire, introduced in the later nineteenth century, obsessed fox-hunters. 'The snake has risen out of the grass and secreted itself in the hedge.'

Still I recall it, that fearful disaster,
The fence where the wire was obscured from the eye;
Gamely they tried it, the mare and the Master,
Gamely they fell, with the hounds in full cry.

Such a sad spectacle, oh! so unsightly,
Mangled and bleeding he lay on the plain.
'Steady!' they gave the word, 'lift him there lightly,
Spread the coat over him, let him remain.'

Peace! it is well, see the white clouds are fleeting,
Over the vale comes the Angel of Death,
Wrapt in such mystery – hush! they are meeting,
The soul and the Angel depart as a breath.

So did he die with his comrades around him;
Dairymaid licked the strong hand as he lay;
Perfect as Master and huntsman we found him,
Now the strong life has gone down to decay.

Farmers, be merciful, pause we implore you,
Pause ere you strengthen your fences with wire,
Mark the fair lives ever passing before you,
Let them ride honestly over the shire.

Strike them not down in the midst of their pleasure
Leave them to ride over England at large,
Leave them to follow the past-time they treasure,
Do not let murder be laid to your charge.

W. Phillpotts Williams, *The Grave in the Vale*, 1894

*G. J. Whyte-Melville (1821–78) to a landowner who had
put up wire :*

I am a Christian man, and bear no malice; but if anyone were to tell me you had got a wasp's nest inside
your breeches, I should be very glad to hear it.

Lord Cardigan's death.

But perhaps the late Lord Cardigan, the last of the
Brudenells, afforded in the hunting-field, as in all other

scenes of life, the most striking example of that 'pluck' which is totally independent of youth, health, strength, or any other physical advantage. The courage that in advanced middle-age governed the steady manoeuvres of Bulganak, and led the death-ride at Balaclava, burned bright and fierce to the end. The graceful seat might be less firm, the tall soldier-like figure less upright, but Mars, one of his last and best hunters, was urged to charge wood and water by the same bold heart at seventy, that tumbled Langar into the Uppingham road over the highest gate in Leicestershire at twenty-six. The foundation of Lord Cardigan's whole character was valour. He loved it, he prized it, he admired it in others, he was conscious and proud of it in himself.

So jealous was he of this chivalrous quality, that even in such a matter of mere amusement as riding across a country, he seemed to attach some vague sense of disgrace to the avoidance of a leap, however dangerous, if hounds were running at the time, and was notorious for the recklessness with which he would plunge into the deepest rivers though he could not swim a stroke!

This I think is to court *real* danger for no sufficient object.

The gallant old cavalry officer's death was in keeping with his whole career. At threescore years and ten he insisted on mounting a dangerous animal that he would not have permitted any friend to ride. What happened is still a mystery. The horse came home without him, and he never spoke again, though he lived till the following day.

G. J. Whyte-Melville, *Riding Recollections*, 1875

It is a terrible fate, when married to a bold rider, to have lost one's nerve. This unfortunate found he funked his fences after a polo accident.

There was but one fence now between Hugh and the road. It was a large bank with furze bushes growing on it, and a small ditch in front of it. Hugh trotted down its whole length with a sick, angry heart, looking for a low place.

'My God!' he said to himself, 'I can't ride at it. It's no good trying.'

One spot seemed to him a trifle lower than the rest, and setting his teeth, he put the horse at it. The effort to command himself and not to pull the horse's head as he came to the jump amounted in its way to agony; he did not know if he were glad or sorry when the grey, soured by the day's misadventures, swerved from the fence and bucketed round the field, pulling hard and trying to get his head down. Hugh stopped him and dismounted. He would not think of what he was going to do, but there was a hard knot in his throat as he walked the grey across the field. He tied the lash of his whip to the reins, and climbing on to the fence, led him over it. The horse followed him as lightly and quietly as a dog, and stood still to let him untie the lash. His hand shook, and he did it awkwardly, while the lump in his throat grew bigger.

The events of the morning were present with him. The jovial breakfast-table at which he had played so sorry a part; the look of the grey horse bucking as he was led round to the door; the cold, sick feeling when the hounds opened on the fox in covert; the look of Glasgow's back as he and the others disappeared over the hill, leaving him stuck at the first fence, engaged in that half-hearted battle with his horse that had resulted in a fall for them both. He hated them all – Bunbury, Glasgow, the road-riding faction, who had volunteered with horrible sympathy to show him the short cuts: he almost hated his wife for the easy confidence in him that he knew he did not deserve.

'I'll get over it,' he said to himself, swearing furiously and futilely. 'After all, this is pretty nearly the first time I've been on a horse since that smash. Damn you, you brute, keep quiet!' This to the grey, who was fidgeting and pulling, with his ears pricked in expectation of anything and everything. 'I've never had a right feel about a horse since that time.' He pulled out his flask and took a drink – his wife had given it to him – and as he put it back he thought, with almost the bitterest pang of all, that she would never understand – that he could never tell her.

The note of the horn struck on his ear, and, looking back through the rain, he saw the hounds coming quietly along the road behind him. Lady Susan and Glasgow were riding in front of them, and he knew that the time had come when he would have to begin to tell lies.

E. Œ. Somerville and M. Ross,
The Silver Fox, 1919

Hunting is enjoyable also because many a run entails a variety of misfortunes for those trying to keep up, misfortunes which, unless badly left behind or out of sight which it is hard to be – there is a witness behind every hedge – can be retailed and are sure to arouse interest if one's family is keen and has been out. Someone has lost a stirrup or staked his horse or has taken the most awful fall and for children this is the first exchange they have on the level of and with their parents, discussion of ideas having only too naturally no appeal on either side. 'They ran hard right up to Volter's and that was where I first saw him being carried on a gate.' But hunting was spoiled for me because I was a coward, my not having a pony when I wanted it being that kind of excuse one uses to explain oneself away . . .

Henry Green, *Pack my Bag*, 1940

Attacks & Defence

Distasteful to the British way of life.

Transport & General Workers' Union, 1957

If there be anyone who is temperamentally opposed to the sport, and would injure it if he could, he is hardly worth considering. His whole outlook would probably be anti-social and un-English.

Lord Willoughby de Broke, MFH, 1925

The attraction of hunting is that it acts on the mind like a poultice on a sore.

Leon Trotsky

Fox-hunting has been attacked on various grounds: Bentham insisted on the rights of animals; poets (Cowper and Wordsworth) and professors (the medievalist E. A. Freeman) that it was an exercise in wanton cruelty; the Evangelicals attacked hunting as a morally degrading and unChristian activity; radicals of all ages because it was, in Cobden's phrase, 'feudal' and confined to the upper classes.

Cock-fights, bull-baiting, hunting hares and foxes, fishing and other amusements of the same kind, necessarily suppose either the absence of reflection or a fund of inhumanity, since they produce most acute sufferings to sensible beings and and most painful and lingering death of which we can form any idea. Why should the law refuse its protection to any sensitive being?

J. Bentham, *The Principles of*
Penal Law (*Works*, ed.
J. Bowring, 1843-8)

Jilly Cooper exposes the mixed motives of the 'antis'.

My attitude towards blood sports is totally irrational. I detest otter and stag hunting. Beagling is far too energetic. Shooting involves too much time shambling about in silence and damp heather, and the only time I went to a bullfight I was so appalled I was sick on a black mantilla.

I must confess, however, that I have a sneaking fondness for fox hunting. I excuse my predilection by telling myself that foxes are vermin and they would have to be shot if they weren't hunted. I have a feeling that people get steamed up about fox hunting because foxes are so beautiful, and if it were a question of chasing snakes or rats down a sewer the anti-blood-sports brigade wouldn't be nearly so clamorous.

I also suspect a touch of class warfare; hunting is popularly seen as an upper-class sport, practised by the rich and seemingly arrogant. It would be more honest to call the dissenters the Anti-Blue-Blood-Sports Brigade.

Sydney Smith was fully aware that the sports of the rich were by convention exempted from the charge of cruelty; those of the poor savagely punished.

Of cruelty to animals let the reader take the following specimen: Running an iron hook in the intestines of an animal; presenting this first animal to another as his food; and then pulling this second creature up and suspending him by the barb in his stomach. Riding a horse till he drops, in order to see an innocent animal

torn to pieces by dogs . . . These cruelties are the
cruelties of the suppressing committee, not of the poor
. . . The first of these cruelties passes under the pretty
name of *angling*; and therefore there can be no harm
in it. The next is *hunting*; and as many of the Vice
Presidents of the Committee hunt, it is not possible
that there can be any cruelty in hunting. A man of
£10,000 a year may worry a fox as much as he pleases,
may encourage the breed of that mischievous animal
on purpose to worry it; and a poor labourer is carried
before a magistrate for paying 6d to see an exhibition
of courage between a dog and a bear.

> A review of the Proceedings for the Society for the
> Suppression of Vice, *Edinburgh Review*, 1809

Bernard Shaw wrote a preface to Killing for Sport
*(1915). He was too intelligent to take the indignation of
humanitarians at its face value. Moreover, since animals*

had to be killed because 'evolution . . . involves a deliberate intentional destruction by the higher forms of life of the lower', why not kill for sport?

In the sports firmly established among us there is much less of this abomination. In fox hunting and shooting, predatory excitement is not a necessary part of the sport, and is indeed abhorred by many who practise it. Inveterate foxhunters have been distressed and put off their hunting for days by happening to see a fox in the last despairing stage of its run from the hounds: a sight which can be avoided, and often is, by the hunters, but which they may happen upon some day when they are not hunting. Such people hunt because they delight in meets and in gallops across country as social and healthy incidents of country life. They are proud of their horsemanship and their craftiness in taking a line. They like horses and dogs and exercise and wind and weather, and are unconscious of the fact that their expensive and well equipped hunting stables and kennels are horse prisons and dog prisons. It is useless to pretend that these ladies and gentlemen are fiends in human form: they clearly are not. By avoiding being in at the death they get all the good out of hunting without incurring the worst of the evil, and so come out with a balance in their favour. There are now so many other pastimes available that the choice of killing is becoming more and more a disgrace to the chooser. The wantonness of the choice is beyond excuse. To kill as the poacher does, to sell or eat the victim, is at least to act reasonably. To kill from hatred or revenge is at least to behave passionately. To kill in gratification of a lust for death is at least to behave villainously. Reason, passion, and villainy are all human. But to kill, being all the time quite a good sort of fellow, merely to pass away the time when there are a dozen harmless ways of doing it equally available, is to behave like an idiot or a silly imitative sheep.

Surely the broad outlook and deepened consciousness which admits all living things to the commonwealth of fellow-feeling, and the appetite for fruitful activity and generous life which come with it, are better than this foolish doing of unamiable deeds by people who are not in the least unamiable.

A day with the antis.

I've always felt slightly guilty about being pro-fox-hunting, so I decided last week to see the other side, and spent a day out with the anti-foxhunting fraternity, or Hunt Saboteurs as they prefer to be called.

On arrival . . . I was given a badge to wear saying Hounds off our Wildlife, and an aerosol can of Anti-Mate to spray on hounds and likely-looking huntsmen.

The Saboteurs had evidently been up half the night unblocking earths and spraying the area with aniseed. 'Sometimes we wave banners saying: "Only rotters hunt otters," ' said a pink-faced girl.

Several magenta-faced colonels and braying ladies on shooting-sticks were giving us dirty looks. Labradors knowingly sat behind the grilles of shooting brakes as though they were about to take confession. A group of men in deer-stalkers and dung-coloured clothes stood grimly beside a Land-Rover.

'Those are the heavies,' whispered Mike. 'They're paid by the hunt to sabotage us.'

They looked very heavy indeed. I was beginning to feel uneasy, when suddenly hounds arrived, tails wagging merrily, and the hunt clattered off in its glory of scarlet coats, top hats and burnished horses.

Few sights can lift the spirit more. I decided one must remain loyal to one's prejudices and surreptitiously removed the Hounds off our Wildlife badge from my coat. Several Antis surged forward spraying the hounds with Anti-Mate.

'Keep your eyes peeled for foxes,' hissed the Chief Saboteur.

Hounds were put into a pale-green larch covert. We parked on the edge of a field above them, and next moment a posse of Saboteurs leapt over the fence and, armed with Anti-Mate, raced across the field, disappearing into the covert.

Pa pa pa pa pa came the tender melancholy note of the horn. 'Oh goodee, I mean, oh dear,' I said hastily, 'they appear to have found a fox.'

'That's Iain,' said his girlfriend proudly. 'He's learnt how to blow the horn as well as any whipper-in.'

Finally we found hounds again in full cry inside the high walls of the Petworth estate. Unable to get at them physically, the Saboteurs launched their toughest offensive. All hell broke loose, as smoke bombs and thunder flashes exploded, foghorns wailed, horns and whistles were blown.

I hid under a holly bush praying. The Saboteurs charged about yelling, screaming, encouraging, slipping on wet leaves, tripping over the long silver roots of the beech trees.

Hounds had evidently gone to pieces – all we could hear from the other side was whimpering, furious bellows and a lively stream of expletives. A Saboteur shinned up the wall to look. 'The Master's lost control,' he crowed, then clambered down hastily as a huntsman's face appeared over the other side, blazingly angry:

'I killed twenty Germans in the last war,' he bellowed 'and all of them were more of a man than you lot.'

'Look,' said a heavy walking over to us, 'why don't you go home? You've completely wrecked our day.' I must say I agreed with him. The Saboteurs seemed to have a marvellous time, playing cops and robbers, spoiling everyone's fun, and feeling virtuous to boot.

As a hunting acquaintance said the other day: 'If they ever abolish hunting, I shall definitely become an Anti.'

Jilly Cooper, *Jolly Superlative*, 1975

Fox-hunters are reluctant to defend their sport on the grounds that it is enjoyable. This would be to talk into the jaws of the antis. Apart from the standard defence that hunting is the most humane method of controlling the fox population and the paradoxical defence that, without the preservation of foxes for hunting, there would be no foxes, they have exalted the hunting field as a training ground for character and the breeding of military virtues.

These inherent qualities of effort and exploit which comprise hunting at its best have meant that it has always been considered a great education, one of the preferred methods of training character. Only in the contemporary period and, within that, only in the most demoralized regions of Europe has an affinity for hunting been held in disesteem.

José Ortega y Gasset, *Meditations on Hunting*

Fox-hunting bred an imperial race.

In sharing the sport of his superiors in rank the young middle-class Englishman began to acquire the virtues and good qualities of a governing race, and to graft on his sturdy common sense the habits of regularity and the business capacity which have always distinguished his own class, the boldness, the dash, and the endurance that are common characteristics of our aristocracy. It is these latter which have served in our own day to help us to create a flourishing province out of a desert, to regenerate an ancient and glorious kingdom, and to rule successfully an immense dependency of mixed races. It is no more defence of a favourite recreation, or excuse for a pursuit in which so many delight, but in a serious spirit of thoughtful deduction from facts, that I claim for fox hunting more particularly that grafting of aristocratic virtues on a democratic polity which is the peculiar source and strength of English character and power of rule.

T. F. Dale, *The History of the Belvoir Hunt*, 1899

The Duke of Wellington hunted in Hampshire and kept a pack of foxhounds in the Peninsula. General Excelmann recognized the daring of English fox-hunting officers in the Napoleonic Wars, but added

The great deficiency is in your officers who seem to be impressed by the conviction that they can dash or ride over everything, as if the art of war were precisely the same as the art of fox hunting.

Quoted in Charles Chenevix-Trench,
A History of Horsemanship, 1970

It promotes psychological stability.

Let me not be accused of saying that by promoting foxhunting you will guarantee perpetual peace. What I do say is that one of the things that contributes to a stable society, and thus indirectly to a state of peace, is psychological health; and I add that pastimes which call to the dark and only partly conscious wild in us, which keep us 'unrepressed', if only by the knowledge that an outlet exists, are essential to psychological well-being. So, in the sense I have indicated, I praise hunting because it is mad.

Christopher Sykes, 'Summing up some memories'
from In Praise of Hunting, 1960

It is an antidote to lust.

When he cometh home he cometh joyfully, for his lord had given him to drink of his good wine at the curée, and when he has come home he shall doff his clothes and his shoes and his hose, and he shall wash his thighs and his legs, and peradventure all his body. And in the meanwhile he shall order well his supper, with wortes (roots) and of the neck of the hart and of other good meats, and good wine or ale. And when he hath well eaten and drunk he shall be glad and well, and well at his ease. And then shall he take the air in the evening of the night, for the great heat that he hath had. And then he shall go and drink and lie in his bed in fair fresh clothes, and shall sleep well and steadfastly all the night without any evil thoughts of any sins, wherefore I say that hunters go into Paradise when they die, and live in this world more joyfully than any other men.

Edward, Duke of York, The Master of Game, c. 1400

It provides a harmless occupation for the upper classes.

Well a chap must do somethin', I always tell chaps,
For if a chap doesn't a chap will collapse,
And a chap keeps as fit as a chap could be wishin'
As long as there's huntin' and shootin' and fishin'.

A. P. Herbert, *Tantivy Towers*, 1931

*When Sebastian Flyte was taking to drink, his mother –
in spite of herself – clung to the idea of the remedial effect
of fox-hunting.*

'. . . I'm afraid there may be an embarrassing situation tonight if Sebastian gets the chance. He's in a bad mood.'

'Oh, a day's hunting will put that all right.'

It was touching to see the faith which everybody put in the value of a day's hunting. Lady Marchmain, who looked in on me during the morning, mocked herself for it with that delicate irony for which she was famous.

'I've always detested hunting,' she said, 'because it seems to produce a particularly gross kind of caddishness in the nicest people. I don't know what it is, but the moment they dress up and get on a horse they become like a lot of Prussians. And so boastful after it. The evenings I've sat at dinner appalled at seeing the men and women I know, transformed into half-awake, self-opinionated, monomaniac louts! . . . and yet, you know – it must be something derived from centuries ago – my heart is quite light today to think of Sebastian out with them. "There's nothing wrong with him really," I say, "he's gone hunting" – as though it were an answer to prayer.'

Evelyn Waugh, *Brideshead Revisited*, 1945

Against the attack that fox-hunting is 'feudal', fox-hunters have maintained that it is 'democratic'.

[103]

The Field is a most agreeable coffee-house, and there is more real society to be met with there than in any other situation in life. It links all classes together, from the Peer to the Peasant. It is the Englishman's peculiar privilege. It is not to be found in any other part of the globe, but in England's true land of liberty – and may it flourish to the end of time!!'

John Hawkes (a friend of Meynell, Master of the Quorn 1753–1800), c. 1808

I even do not hesitate to assert that so long as fox-hunting endures, so long will all the classes of English society be safe together: the high from the blights of envy and the spoliation of rapacity, the low from the iron hand of oppression and the insolent spurn of contempt.

G. F. Underhill, *A Century of English Foxhunting*, 1900

Here is Otho Paget writing in 1900:

One of the best features of hunting is that it gives all classes a chance of meeting on terms of equality. In the hunting field all men are equal with the exception of the master and the huntsman – they should be absolute autocrats. The peer must take a back seat if the butcher with a bold heart can pound him over a big fence.

Hunting

We make no comment on the following extravaganza.

I would ask whether, in fact, a fox-hunter is a brute. Was Charles Kingsley a brute? Is Mr Masefield a brute? . . . Is Lord Halifax debased? Great Viceroy, great Churchman, great Foreign Secretary – and yet a Master of Harriers and Foxhounds of many years standing, and the father of two Masters of Foxhounds.

Far from having a debasing, brutalizing effect, surely fox-hunting is an influence of moral value? Does it not take men and women away from the filth and vice of the towns into the cleanness of the countryside? No man who is not fit, physically, can enjoy a hunt; no man who is fit physically can be really unfit morally. Fox-hunting is completely democratic – far more democratic, far less snobbish, than any other sport, probably than any game. 'Tell me a man's a Fox-hunter, and I loves him at once' – whether I am a Duke and he is a chimney-sweep. Fox-hunting is the least selfish of all sports, and demands as much team-spirit as any game; for one man can, in a second, ruin the pleasure of five hundred. Fox-hunting calls for real physical courage. Fox-hunters are, frequently, almost too fond of their dogs and their horses. Are they 'brutes'? It might, in passing, do his cause no harm, if the fox-hunter were to point out to his opponent that comparatively few of the semi-intoxicated 'bright young things' whose portraits appear, taken, admittedly, at Hunt Balls, in the society press from week to week are hunting people; rather they are the social riff-raff of the towns, whose minds and bodies could well do with a cleansing dose of fox-hunting.

David Brock, *The Foxhunter's Weekend Book*, 1939

The myth of fox-hunting as a democratic institution has been exposed by David Itzkowitz.

The great attractiveness of this ideal lay in the fact that, though it was simple and straightforward on the surface, it was sufficiently ambiguous to be used to justify a wide range of opinions and practices. It enabled hunting to maintain an image at one and the same time as the most aristocratic and the most egalitarian of English institutions. It enabled what was never more than a small minority of the population to expect that everyone else in the countryside would order his interests so as to foster the amusement of that minority. What is more remarkable is that that expectation was fulfilled . . . Hunting people never quite resolved the conflict between the image of hunting as a sport of gentlemen and as a sport open to all the public.

Peculiar Privilege, 1977

But there are those British people for whom fox-hunting remains a passion, a poetry, and a mystique.

The dusk is down on the river meadows
The moon is climbing above the fir,
The lane is crowded with creeping shadows,
The gorse is only a distant blur.
The last of the light is almost gone,
But hark! They're running!
    They're running on!

The count of the years is steadily growing;
The Old give way to the eager Young;
Far on the hill is the horn still blowing,
Far on the steep are the hounds still strung.
Good men follow the good men gone;
And hark! They're running!
    They're running on.

W. H. Ogilvie, *They're Running On*, 1922

AU REVOIR

◈ Acknowledgements ◈

The editors and publishers gratefully acknowledge permission to use copyright material in this book:

Henry Blythe: From *Skittles* (Hart-Davis, 1970). Copyright 1950 Henry Blythe. By permission of Anthony Sheil Associates Ltd.

David Brock: From *The Foxhunter's Weekend Book*, originally published by Seeley Service & Company Ltd. Reproduced with permission of F. Warne (Publishers) Ltd.

Maurice Collis: From *Somerville and Ross* (Faber, 1968). By permission of the publisher.

Jilly Cooper: From *Jolly Superlative* (Eyre Methuen, 1975). By permission of the author and the publisher.

Jimmy Edwards: From 'Rushing their Fences' in *In Praise of Hunting* (ed. David James and W. Stephens, Hollis & Carter, 1960). By permission of the publisher.

Lady Augusta Fane: From *Chit Chat*. By permission of the Earl of Stradbroke.

José Ortega y Gasset: From *Meditations on Hunting*. By permission of Soledad Ortega for the Fundación José Ortega y Gasset, Madrid.

Henry Green: From *Pack My Bag* (1940). By permission of the Author's Literary Estate and The Hogarth Press Ltd.

Max Hastings: From an article in the *Observer*, 23 November 1980. By permission of the author.

A. P. Herbert: From *Tantivy Towers*. By permission of A. P. Watt Ltd., for Lady Herbert.

David Itzkowitz: From *Peculiar Privilege* (The Harvester Press Ltd.) By permission of the publisher.

Lord Knutsford: From 'Hunting and the Hound' in *In Praise of Hunting* (ed. David James and W. Stephens, Hollis & Carter, 1960). By permission of the publisher.

John Masefield: From 'Reynard the Fox', copyright 1919, and renewed 1947 by John Masefield, from *Poems*. By permission of The Society of Authors as the literary representative of the Estate of John Masefield, and of Macmillan Publishing Co., Inc.

T. G. Paget: From *The History of the Althorp and Pytchley*. By permission of R. T. Paget.

Anthony Powell: From *From a View to a Death* (Heinemann, 1933). By permission of the publisher and of David Higham Associates Ltd.

Siegfried Sassoon: From *Memoirs of a Fox-Hunting Man* (1928). By permission of Faber & Faber Ltd., and the K. S. Giniger

ACKNOWLEDGEMENTS

Company, Inc., New York, in association with Stackpole Books, Harrisburg.

G. B. Shaw: From *Killing for Sport*. By permission of The Society of Authors on behalf of the Bernard Shaw Estate.

Christopher Sykes: From 'Summing up some memories' in *In Praise of Hunting* (ed. David James and W. Stephens, Hollis & Carter, 1960). By permission of the publisher.

Frank Watson: From *In the Pink* (H. F. & G. Witherby Ltd.)

Evelyn Waugh: From *Brideshead Revisited*. Copyright 1944, 1945 by Evelyn Waugh. Copyright © renewed 1972, 1973 by Mrs Laura Waugh. Reprinted by permission of A. D. Peters & Co. Ltd., and Little, Brown, Inc.

John Wyndham: From *Wyndham and Children First* (Macmillan, 1968). By permission of the publisher.

While every effort has been made to secure permission, we may have failed in a few cases to trace the copyright holder. We apologize for any apparent negligence.

The illustrations in this book were taken from the following sources: *The Field, The Fox Hunt, and The Farm* (London, n.d.); Nimrod, *Hunting Reminiscences* (London, 1843); R. S. Surtees (with illustrations by John Leech), *Mr. Sponge's Sporting Tour* (London, 1853), *Handley Cross* (London, 1854), *Ask Mamma* (London, 1858), *Plain or Ringlets?* (London, 1860).

Index